Ethical Leadership and the Community College: Paradigms, Decision-Making, and Praxis

A Volume in:
Transformative Leadership in Postsecondary Education

Series Editors
Carlos Nevarez
J. Luke Wood

Transformative Leadership in Postsecondary Education

Series Editors

Carlos Nevarez
California State University, Sacramento

J. Luke Wood
San Diego State University

The Curriculum and Pedagogy Group

Ethical Leadership and the Community College:
Paradigms, Decision-Making, and Praxis (2014)
By J. Luke Wood and Carlos Nevarez

Ethical Leadership and the Community College: Paradigms, Decision-Making, and Praxis

J. Luke Wood
Carlos Nevarez

INFORMATION AGE PUBLISHING, INC.
Charlotte, NC • www.infoagepub.com

Library of Congress Cataloging-in-Publication Data

The CIP data for this book can be found on the Library of Congress website (loc.gov).

Paperback: 978-1-62396-809-0
Hardcover: 978-1-62396-810-6
eBook: 978-1-62396-811-3

Printed in the United States of America

CONTENTS

Feb 19

v

PART III

PROBLEM-SOLVING THROUGH CASE STUDIES

ACKNOWLEDGEMENTS

First and foremost, we would like to thank our families for their support and encouragement. We would like to acknowledge and thank all of the case study contributors for this book who shared their experiences and insights. It allowed the authors of this book to contextualize the content in practice. We would like to thank the various leaders who shared their views on ethical leadership. Also, we would like thank our colleagues and graduate students who aided us in various ways on this project. We would like to acknowledge Cecelia M. Krek and Marissa Vasquez Urias for providing technical support, and George F. Johnson of Information Age for his contribution to advancing the body of literature on community colleges. It is our hope that the efforts of all involved with the development of this book can lead to better ethical leadership practices. This ensures everyone's interest are advanced and protected.

Ethical Leadership and the Community College: Paradigms, Decision-Making, and Praxis,
pages vii.
Copyright © 2014 by Information Age Publishing
All rights of reproduction in any form reserved.

PART I

LAYING THE FOUNDATIONS FOR ETHICAL PRACTICE

CHAPTER 1

ETHICS, DECISION-MAKING, AND PRAXIS

justice
critique
care local community

This chapter discusses the foundational, conceptual, interpersonal, and practical dispositions needed to develop ethical leaders. Then, four paradigms for ethical decision-making (ethic of justice, critique, care, and local community) are critically examined. The chapter closes with the presentation of an ethical case study framework aimed at arming leaders with the analytical tools to situate problems in context of ethical principles, while guiding problem resolution.

When reading this chapter, consider the following questions:

- What are the components necessary for developing ethical leaders from a holistic perspective?
- What are the four-primary ethical paradigms? How do they differ?
- What are the benefits using a theoretical decision-making approach for resolving moral dilemmas?
- What are the primary steps in problem-solving?

Ethical Leadership and the Community College: Paradigms, Decision-Making, and Praxis, pages 3–11.

foundation (

This book is designed to aid community college leaders in becoming ethical leaders. This aim is essential, as ethical leadership is needed to address the continual ethical quandaries and persistent leadership dilemmas (e.g., funding, governance, accountability, shifting student demographics) facing public postsecondary education in the current era. When leaders are fully committed to the ideals that underscore public education (e.g., public good, access, social mobility, civic engagement) and accept the notion that their role as leaders is to be a servant to others, ethical leadership serves as a roadmap to guide their decisions, actions, and advocacy.

foundational conceptual interpersonal practical

This volume serves as a comprehensive resource in articulating the foundational, conceptual, interpersonal, and practical dispositions of the critical need to develop leaders with high moral aptitudes. These four elements serve as the cornerstone of the authors approach to professional development for ethical leadership and decision-making, as well as the analytical structure of this text. The foundational context provided in this volume focuses on the socio-historical and theoretical context of the field of ethics in the community college and ethical paradigms described. The conceptual context refers to core definitions as well as applicability of these concepts to community college practice. The interpersonal contexts focuses on 'knowing thyself' through introspective inventories that allows leaders to critically examine their prior assumptions, dispositions and propensity towards certain decision-making approaches. Moreover, leaders can use this information as a frame of reference to determine the next steps for their own professional development in becoming more well-rounded ethical thinkers and decision-makers. The practical context enables leaders to engage in praxis (theory to practice connections) whereby their applied practice is informed by ethical theories and models. The practical context employs the use of case studies written by college and university leaders who have extensive experiential knowledge and keen understanding of problem solving in light of ethical principles.

This theoretical decision-making approach allows leaders to consider how the use of frameworks, different from those that they would normally acclimate to, would look like in practice. Our goal is that leaders would use the conceptual, interpersonal and practical contexts provided in this volume to stretch themselves intellectually. In doing so, as shown in Figure 1.1, the culminating results of the four-fold development process is the creation of leaders who are better decision-makers, problem solvers, critically introspective, and employ theory in practical contexts (praxis). We firmly believe that the aforementioned process will result in better leaders who are cognitively and affectively mature to address the complex, multidimensional, and dynamic nature of leadership challenges in the community college.

In contextualizing the vast body of literature on ethics, the focus of this volume, as illustrated in Figure 1.2, is to outline four primary ethical paradigms; ethic of justice, ethic of critique, ethic of care, and ethic of local community. While it is recognized that additional ethical models, frameworks, styles, and ap-

praxis = theory to practice connections

becoming more well rounded ethical thinkers and decision-makers

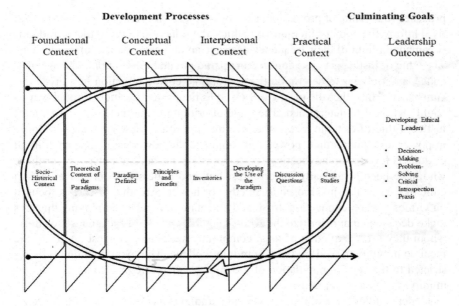

FIGURE 1.1. Four-Fold Developmental Process.

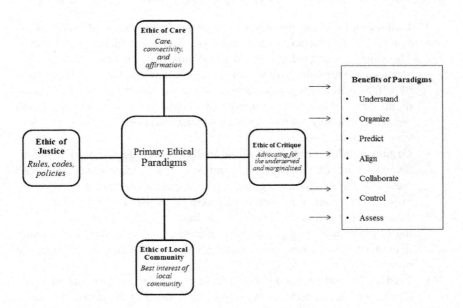

FIGURE 1.2. Four Primary ethical paradigms

proaches (e.g., ethic of profession, axiology, golden rule, and categorical imperative) inform the body of literature on ethics, the selection of these four paradigms was made in light of their frequency of usage among community college leaders. The ethic of justice is a decision-making paradigm that relies upon existing rules, codes, and policies to determine the appropriate course of action in a given circumstance. Thus, the rule of law is viewed as the primary vehicle through which 'right' actions are determined. The ethic of critique is antithetical to an ethic of justice. Ethic-of-critique leaders believe that the rule of law is created by those in power to maintain their power and subjugate the powerless. Thus, an ethic of critique is focused on advocating for the interests, needs, and outcomes for those who have been historically underrepresented and underserved in education. An ethic of care is also juxtaposed to an ethic of justice. An ethic of care is focused on virtues of care, connection, trust, and affirmation. Leaders employing this lens make decisions that prioritize the well-being, dignity, and best-interests of those whom they serve. An ethic of local community seeks the 'greatest good' for the local community served by the community college. The local community is restricted to the service population of the college, therefore prioritizing the 'community' in name 'community' college.

Understanding each of the four ethical paradigms has several benefits for leadership. We believe that the benefits for understanding ethical theory are similar to that of having an advanced knowledge of leadership theories (see Nevarez & Wood, 2010). An advanced understanding of ethical theory allows leaders to:

- **Understand.** Ethical paradigms provide leaders with an enhanced understanding of approaches that they and other leaders use in making decisions. Therefore, understanding ethical paradigms (e.g., justice, critique, care, and local community) allows for leaders to have a better understanding of self, as well as those around them. An astute awareness of ethical paradigms can enable leaders to better make connections between actions and behaviors that may not be overtly conceptualized as ethical as in fact being very ethical in nature.
- **Organize.** Ethical paradigms allow leaders to consider the myriad of contextual factors and concerns relevant to a given circumstance. This can prevent leaders from making decisions that are mono-dimensional and uninformed by considering factors that were previously ignored in their decision-making process. This can provide leaders with a holistic understanding of phenomena (e.g., competing interests, people, power) surrounding dilemmas; thereby lending to better and more informed critical-analytic problem-solving.
- **Predict.** By understanding ethical theories that are often employed in decision-making, leaders can become more attuned to the decision-making considerations and processes employed by others around them. This can allow leaders to better predict the core concerns and actions of other lead-

ers before they occur. In essence, a leader's predictability is guided by the contextual nuances and structural tendencies that serve as a 'mental roadmap' to foreseeing how issues will be 'played out.' In any leadership circumstance, being able to predict the actions of others provides an edge in advocating for the best interests of the students, personnel, and communities served by community colleges.

- **Align**. In gaining an advanced understanding of considerations and being able to predict the actions of others, leaders with an awareness of ethical decision-making can consider the most appropriate course of action in maneuvering resources, people, policies, and structures to facilitate positive outcomes. For example, if a leader is prone to making decisions based on the rule of law (ethic of justice), another leader can consider how to revise processes, codes, and procedures in advance of making decisions that will likely be impacted by existing policy.
- **Collaborate**. Leaders who understand the typical decision-making paradigms employed by their colleagues can use this information to determine appropriate collaborations in advocating for the best interests of their institutions. Given the dynamic nature of problems and issues faced by college leaders, leaders can consider both within and between paradigm collaborations to facilitate the best course of action in a given circumstance. Simply put, ethical awareness allows leaders to build more effectively and leverage partnerships.
- **Control**. Ultimately, the aforementioned benefits of understanding the ethical decision-making processes of oneself and others can empower leaders to have greater levels of control and influence in organizations typified by inconsistency, fluidity, and competing interests. Given the increasingly bureaucratic and tense nature of leadership in community colleges, greater levels of control can lead to better organizational outcomes. Moreover, added control provides the leader and their followers with greater professional stability and credibility, both of which are integral to their success.
- **Assess**. Leaders often tend to gravitate towards one ethical paradigm versus another. An understanding of multiple paradigms enables leaders to better assess the course of action they made when facing an ethical dilemma. Assessment allows for an establishment of intended outcomes and a mechanism to measure goal attainment. This assessment enables a leader to determine whether or not they took the most appropriate course of action. This approach will empower leaders to hone their ethical decision-making capacities to become more well-rounded leaders when addressing future problems.

The authors present the four ethical paradigms (e.g., justice, critique, care, and local community) with the understanding that these paradigms are often used in isolation in common practice. We assert that a unified approach is needed where leaders are well-versed in all paradigms and consider each when making decisions. This may result in decisions that are more reflective than reactive. To be clear, we are not advocating situational ethics (where the right course of action is made based on the contingencies of each individual situation). Such an approach would lead to a directionless and purposeless leader. We believe that leaders should consider and employ each of the four ethical paradigms, but that their practice should be undergirded by core virtues. Virtues are similar to values in that they are highly esteemed values. For example, leaders often value exercise, eating healthy, a beautiful campus, up-front parking, etc. However, if any of these were not fully evident, the dignity of the leader would not be sacrificed. In contrast, *virtues* are highly esteemed values that leaders cannot be without. Common examples of virtues include: respect, patience, justice, longsuffering, and fortitude. The loss of any of these would lessen the dignity of leaders and the organizations they serve. We assert that, specific to community college leadership, five core virtues are needed: diversity, social justice, integrity, accountability, and compassion. We believe that these virtues should underscore a unified ethical approach, serving as a foundation for ethical decision-making. By employing these five virtues, leaders will have a center of directed focus that will allow them to maintain their commitment to serving and advancing the lives of the students, staff, and communities they serve.

ETHICAL CASE STUDY FRAMEWORK

Problem-solving is a skillset developed through critical thinking, experimental learning, and possessing an operational ability to address competing subtleties influencing institutional problems. What follows is a case study framework aimed at arming leaders with the analytical tools to situate problems in context of ethical principles (see Nevarez & Wood, 2012 for a full articulation of this framework). This empowers leaders to understand comprehensively the entire scope of the problem while giving leaders the ability to select the best approach (e.g., justice, critique, care, and local community) to problem-solve. Although the case study framework is presented in a step-by-step frame of reference, leaders should view the framework as multidimensional and dynamic in nature. In this manner, leaders can capture the unpredictability inherently involved with problem-solving. Leaders should keep an open mind and expect unforeseen circumstances to originate. Approaching problem-solving in this manner allows leaders to have a better sense of control, and be effective in solving institutional dilemmas. When encountering an ethical dilemma or resolving the case studies in this text, leaders should follow the steps below in resolving the issue at hand.

Step 1:   Assume the role of an ethical leader by using ethical principles in problem-solving.

Step 2:   Identify the relevant factors impacting the case:

- Setting—Describe the setting and how the environment may be influencing the case. Example questions: Where is the institution located? What are the characteristics of the institution and its affiliates?
- People—Identify the primary stakeholders involved in the case.
- Example questions: Who are the key individuals? What is the relationship between them? What are the political motives of the stakeholders? Are there other underlying interests involved?
- Special Circumstances—Document the special circumstance or 'X' factors associated with the case.
- Example questions: What are unique and underlying nuances in need of consideration? What established work culture informs acceptable behavior? What are the formal and informal power dynamics?

Step 3: Identify the underlying case problem(s). Note that many cases have more than one peripheral problem, but typically there is only one root problem.

- Example questions: What is(are) the primary problem(s) at play? What are the secondary issues at hand? What is the directional relationship between the primary and secondary issues?

Step 4: Analyze the case through the four ethical paradigms to determine potential courses of action in decision-making.

- The *ethic of justice* is a decision-making paradigm that relies upon existing rules, codes, and policies to determine the appropriate course of action in a given circumstance.
- The *ethic of critique* is focused on advocating for the interests, needs, and outcomes for those who have been historically underrepresented and underserved in education.
- The *ethic of care* is focused on virtues of care, connection, trust, and affirmation.
- The *ethic of local* community seeks the 'greatest good' for the local community served by the community college.

Step 5: Identify a resolution to the case or problem at hand. Refer to all steps in considering multiple courses of action and make a determination. Potential courses of action include:

- **Solve.** Determine a course of action that will eliminate the problem(s) in totality.
- **Resolve.** Determine a short-term course of action that is not ideal as it may not fully remedy the issue.

- **Postpone**. Defer making a decision at this time (typically there is a need to consult further individuals, elicit additional data, or let the issue 'drag' on).
- **Redirect**. Pass on the problem to another individual, department, or group.
- **No action**. Opt not to make any decision in order to let the problem resolve itself.

Step 6: Evaluate the course of action. After making a determination, evaluate the course of action taken and its effect on the issue. Reflection should inform how the leader addresses future problems. Dependent upon the results, the issue should be vetted again across the six steps.

DISCUSSION QUESTIONS

- Based upon the cursory coverage of the ethic of justice, critique, care, and local community, what ethical paradigm(s) do you believe you will likely align with?
- This chapter noted that there are differences between virtues and values in that virtues are highly esteemed values. What are five core virtues (e.g., patience, diversity, integrity, honesty, and compassion) that you personally ascribe to? How might different perspectives on virtues influence leadership dynamics?
- A six-step model of ethical decision-making was described in this chapter. In reflecting upon your own leadership practice, what steps (if any) do you typically take when making decisions?

DEFINITIONS

Conceptual context refers to core definitions as well as applicability of these concepts to community college practice.

Ethic of Care is focused on virtues of care, connection, trust, and affirmation.

Ethic of Critique is focused on advocating for the interests, needs, and outcomes for those who have been historically underrepresented and underserved in education.

Ethic of Justice is a decision-making paradigm that relies upon existing rules, codes, and policies to determine the appropriate course of action in a given circumstance.

Ethic of Local Community seeks the 'greatest good' for the local community served by the community college.

Foundational context focuses on the socio-historical and theoretical context of the field of ethics.

Interpersonal contexts focuses on 'knowing thyself' through introspective inventories that allow leaders to critically examine their own ethical assumptions, dispositions and propensities.

Praxis practice informed, guided, and propelled by theory.

Practical context refers to engaging leaders in praxis (theory to practice connections) whereby their applied practice is informed by ethical theories and models.

Virtues highly esteemed values that leaders cannot be without.

CHAPTER 2

ETHICS, LEADERSHIP, AND THE LAW

This chapter covers core concepts and definitions including: ethics, morality, leadership, and ethical leadership. The notion of a moral compass is discussed as a tool for guiding and centering leaders' decision-making. This chapter concludes with a discussion of the relationship between ethics and the law, along with a related discussion on varying perspectives on the origin of law.

When reading this chapter, consider the following questions:

- What is the difference between ethics and morality?
- Is leadership an inherently ethical enterprise?
- What is a moral compass, and how can it aid leaders in decision-making?
- Are ethics and the law always one in the same?
- What are varying perspectives on the origins of law? How might these perspectives lead to differing perceptions on the relationship between ethics and the law?

Infusing ethics into one's role as a leader is a process, and a difficult one at that. It requires a desire to be an ethical being: a personal, organizational, and commu-

Ethical Leadership and the Community College: Paradigms, Decision-Making, and Praxis, pages 13–21.
Copyright © 2014 by Information Age Publishing

nity-driven aspiration to reach a higher standard of daily operation and decision-making. Then, it necessitates an open-minded exposure to varying frameworks, theories, and models of ethics; some of which may seem, and perhaps are, overly abstract. It then demands an honest and deep introspection into one's known and unknown values as well as a commitment to wrestle intellectually with the validity, usefulness, and meaning of those values. Through this course of action, a leader's current method of practice in decision making is weighed against alternative practices. In a way, the process of becoming an ethical leader is akin to a continual personal renaissance (French word for *rebirth*), as a renewed leader with more conscious values and purpose is manifested, a gradual awakening to new (and hopefully better) ways of serving students. The arduous process of becoming a more ethical leader is not unlike other difficult journeys in our lives in that the experience of the process is meaningful and the reward of the journey is beneficial.

Perceptions of ethics can vary greatly based upon one's political ideology, culture, religion, and other contextual factors. Thus, in becoming an ethical leader, it is important to expect that others will challenge your moral being as their own view of what is 'right' may differ from your own. This highlights the need to have a strong moral base that is anchored in self-awareness. *Self-awareness* refers to one's knowledge of one's own assumptions, dispositions, values, and mores as it relates to what is, and is not, ethical. Often, the cardinal decision-making process, whether conscious or unconscious, employed in making ethical decisions is rooted in religious and spiritual value-systems. However, every person is different, and their adherence to these values systems differs greatly. Thus, what does and does not constitute ethics, morality, and ethical leadership can serve as a point of disagreement. In setting the context for this volume, the following sections overview foundational definitions for these terms.

TOWARDS A DEFINITION OF ETHICS

What is right? What is wrong? How should I operate in this situation? All of these questions fall within the study of ethics. As a result, ethics permeates every aspect of leaders' personal and professional lives. It is imbedded with decision-making on issues such as academic programming, institutional advancement, personnel matters, college finance, student services, and institutional policy. The ubiquitous nature of ethical considerations in community colleges and four-year institutions requires that leaders in these institutions have a clearer understanding of what constitutes ethics. A number of definitions of ethics exist, likely the sheer volume of these definitions are due to the complexity of issues and topics which can be addressed under the umbrella of ethics. Further, each definition highlights the importance of one or more concepts central to varying perspectives on ethics. Consider the following definitions of ethics:

> Ethics "refers to standards of behavior that tell us how human beings ought to act in the many situations in which they find themselves" (Velasquez et al., 2009, para 2).

"Ethics consists of the systematic and critical study of man's moral beliefs: it is the *theory* of morals, the attempt to make our moral beliefs clear, self-consistent, and consistent with the facts we know about man and the world" (Dewey, Gramlich, & Loftsgordon, 1961, p. 1).

"Ethics is the study of what constitutes a moral life; an ethics is a summary, systematic statement of what is necessary to live a moral life" (Starratt, 2004, p. 5).

"The study of ethics is about what we should do and what we should be" (Ciulla, 2003, p. xi).

Within each of these definitions, several words and phrases appear that capture the essence of ethics: "standards of behavior," "theory of morals," "system and critical study," "study of morals," "summary, systematic statement," and "what we should do." With these core notions in mind, *ethics* is defined as the systematic, critical, and summative study of standards needed for moral living. Key to this definition of ethics is the view that ethics is the creation of a standard. It is the thought process, conceptualization, and study of what constitutes a moral life. This suggests that the word ethics, in and of itself, does not refer to an action where leaders' ethical convictions serve to guide their behavior. Instead, ethics is, at its core, a theory of righteous living. You may ask how ethics or theory can be separated from practice. However, this artificial barrier between theory and practice is in many ways to be expected. Often in our lives we have standards (e.g., rules, laws, codes, principles, and values) in which we believe. But belief in standards doesn't mean that they are actualized all the time. For example, many leaders would argue that truth is a standard to which they subscribe. Nevertheless, few would maintain that they have never lied. Whether in the form of an over-exaggeration, slight skew or omission of facts, or outright lie, all leaders' have at times (possibly more than some would like to admit) missed their standard.

While ethics is the standard, morality is ethics in action. *Morality* is adhering to one's ethical standards through thoughts and behaviors. In a similar vein, Starratt (2004) states that "morality is the living, the acting out of ethical beliefs and commitments" (p. 5). Thus, morality is evident when the leaders' moral convictions lead them to action. Though this text delineates between ethics (theory) and morality (practice), it should be noted that these words are often used interchangeably in daily life. If someone is referred to as an ethical person or a moral person the connotation usually suggests the same meaning. It connotes that a person lives out their moral standard. In fact, some *ethicians* (those who study ethical and moral philosophy) avoid separating the two concepts; instead, arguing that there is little or no difference between these terms (see Beckner, 2004). This text avoids blurring the differences between these concepts.

UNDERSTANDING ETHICAL LEADERSHIP

To understand what it means to be an ethical leader, one must first understand leadership. Nevarez & Wood (2010) define a *leadership* as "influencing and inspiring others beyond desired outcomes" (p. 57). This definition implies that being a leader is not necessarily associated with a position of power such as an administrative appointment (e.g., president, vice president, provost, dean, director, or coordinator). A person who guides others towards a mutual goal is a leader, regardless of their post. In essence, leadership is a much more organic enterprise. Leadership can arise from any position within an institution; administrators, faculty, staff, students and even community members can lead in community colleges. Similar to the difference between ethics (theory) and morality (practice), leadership also signifies an action or a practice. Thus, when one combines the words ethics and leadership there is an assumption that one is fulfilling their ethical standards through the practice of leadership. With this in mind, *ethical leadership* is the practice of inspiring others towards a desired outcome while exemplifying an established standard for moral living. When leadership is involved, the act of inspiring others insinuates both a personal and professional commitment to ethical standards as well as inspiring others to a higher standard of moral living. Thus, it is both being moral and encouraging morality among others.

TOWARDS A MORAL COMPASS

A perennial topic of discussion in ethics leadership courses examines the infamous rule of Adolph Hitler. Students are asked to consider whether Hitler was a 'good' leader. Invariably, this question will draw polarized perceptions of what constitutes leadership. Some students will say that Hitler was a poor leader. They will point to the terror spread by the Nazi regime against political opponents, the systematic extermination of the Jews and other groups in the Holocaust, and the widespread death and destruction that resulted from World War II. Some students will reluctantly say that Hitler was a good leader, but that it is difficult to state his success given that he used his ability for such evil ends. Still, others will defiantly state that he was a stellar leader. These individuals will point to his powerful oratory abilities, Germany's military might, and the strength of the Nazi party. However, they will admit that while he was a powerful 'leader,' he certainly was not an ethical leader.

> Leadership without ethics is manipulation and coercion, not leadership. While Hitler may have held a position of formal authority he was not a leader. Leadership and power or positional authority can often be misconceived. While we have stated that a person who guides others towards a mutual goal is a leader, regardless of their post, leaders should illustrate a sense of stewardship and responsibility that is integrated into their efforts. At a minimum, the mutual goal for which the leader and followers seek to obtain should avoid the destruction of the individuals and entities under their influence. Consider the following metaphor:

Leadership without ethics is like a captain of a ship that has lost its way, battered by the waves of the sea, and barreling without concern towards the rocks of shore. Every second on this course moves the captain, crew, and ship closer and closer to their destruction. In such circumstances, the only way to avert danger is to regain course as fast as possible, to turn the ship in the proper direction. What is the most important tool that a captain has to regain course? A compass.

A compass is a tool used to guide the captain, to help him or her take the proper direction. Like the captain of the ship, educational leaders (e.g., Presidents, Vice Presidents, Deans, Program Directors, and faculty) without some sort of guide, share the inevitable fate of a captain who is unable to regain course, to meet their end. Without an ethical foundation, their leadership is nothing more than meaningless political posturing. Their ships (community college districts, institutions, programs, and classrooms) remain on a course of destruction. To avert this course, they also need a tool to guide their way. They need, what educational ethicists call, a 'moral compass.' With this in mind, Dalton, Crosby, Valente, and Eberhardt (2009) state the following:

> A compass points the way to some known objective or goal and is used when one is uncertain about current position or direction. A moral compass points the way to what is right or good when one is uncertain about the right thing to do in any situation. A moral compass utilizes established ethical benchmarks and decision-making criteria to point the way to one's moral responsibility in specific situations.

In essence, a *moral compass* is a personal framework of rules, principles, and virtues that guide one's actions, beliefs, and decision-making. The existence and usage of a moral compass distinguishes a moral leader from others. Moral leaders

FIGURE 2.1. Moral Compass

employ their moral compass both when facing difficult ethical dilemmas and in everyday life. This allows them to steer their programs, planning, and institutions in their intended direction. As a result, aspiring and current community college leaders should see leadership and ethics as concepts that cannot be separated. As such, helping college administrators develop a moral compass is paramount to their success. Figure 2.1 illustrates a moral compass focused on developing the leader's use of an ethic of justice, critique, care, and local community to help inform their decision-making. These frames (among others) are viewed as enhancing the decision-making lens of leaders from a moral perspective. Given the increasingly litigious and bureaucratic nature of public postsecondary education, a common framework used in shaping a leader's moral compass is the law. In the next section, we explore how this approach may not always be the most appropriate.

ETHICS AND THE LAW: ONE IN THE SAME?

If a leader upholds the law, have they acted ethically? Or stated differently, if a leader violates the law, have they performed an unethical act? The defining line may not be as clear as one would hope. To assume that breaking or adhering to the law is ethical supposes that the laws under which leaders must abide are 'right' or 'good.' Unfortunately, there is one major problem in applying this level of confidence in law. Laws are created by people and are, therefore, subject to human frailty and misgivings. Some would even argue that laws are created by the powerful to maintain their superiority over the powerless. It is clear that laws are more of a reflection of societal values than of moral truths. For example, slavery, Jim Crow laws, housing discrimination, and miscegenation laws have all, at one time or another, been legal practices in the United States; however, many would maintain that these laws were unethical.[1] Similarly, supporting the Underground Railroad during the era of slavery, civil disobedience during the civil rights movement, and hiding Jews in safe houses in Nazi Germany were all illegal practices, but most would view these practices as ethical. Consider the following examples pertinent to community college leaders:

- It may be legal to assign purposely a difficult teaching schedule to a faculty member who has challenged the authority of the campus administration; however it *may* not be ethical.
- It may be legal for a campus leader to cheat on his/her spouse; however it is not ethical.

---

[1] There is a branch of legal studies called critical legal studies as well as a branch of policy analysis referred to as critical policy studies that address how law and policy have and continue to be used to subjugate minorities, women, the poor, etc. (see Alemán, 2007).

- It may be legal for a campus president to implement a special administrative hire and avoid interviewing other potential candidates for a particular post; however it *may* not be ethical.
- It may be legal for an administrator to lie, or tell a partial truth, to the faculty senate to obtain their approval or support on an administrative measure; however it is not ethical.
- It may be legal for a provost to let go (fire) a number of staff simply for the purpose of reopening their positions to hire them back, or even new employees, at a lower pay rate; however it is *likely* unethical.

It is difficult to provide examples of one engaging in illegal behavior which is ethical because to do so could encourage the opposite of this book's intention. However, if we substitute 'policy' for 'law,' more appropriate illustrations can be presented. Consider the following: A dean allowing a student to register many days after the final deadline may be against a college's policy; however it *may* be ethical. Or, a program director allowing a staff member to drive a student home, which may violate a college's transit policy and open up the institution to possible litigation in the case of a crash, may be against policy; however it could certainly be ethical. Or, not giving a student a failing grade for an egregious violation of an institution's academic honesty (plagiarism) policy may be against school policy; however using this instance as a teachable moment *may* be both more fruitful and ethical. It is clear, that numerous instances of violating or upholding of established standards of law, policy, and procedure could be provided which could or could not be ethical. Thus, it is important for leaders to view ethics as a separate concept unrelated to law and/or policy. Partially, the view on the relationship between law and ethics is centered on one's view of the origin of law(s). The next section explores differing perspectives on this topic.

ORIGIN OF LAWS (DIVINE LAW, LA NATURAL LAW, SOCIAL CONTRACT)

There are three primary views on the origin of laws, codes, and commandments. *Divine law* suggests that laws originate from a divine source (e.g., God, or a supernatural deity). An example of this would be the Ten Commandments. Many individuals, especially those from a Judeo-Christian religious tradition, believe the Ten Commandments have been given to mankind by God. Thus, there is a need to follow these laws in order to adhere to God's will. Another perspective of the origin of law is that of Natural Law. *Natural law* is the perspective that rules and laws originate from nature; the *natural* or inherent drive for the human race to continue and thrive. For example, a law which advocates against killing would be seen as important, because if everyone committed murder, then the human race or species would cease to exist. The third perspective of the origin of laws is a social contract. The concept of a social contract has been proffered by intellectuals such as Thomas Hobbes, John Locke, and Jean-Jacques Rousseau (among many oth-

ers). A *social contract* suggests that laws originate from the societal level through individuals who give up their certain innate laws to the state, in exchange for a social order.

It is important to understand that individuals can maintain multiple perspectives on this topic. For example, one could believe that certain laws originate from divine law (God); whereas others originate from a social contract. Further, individuals can have divergent opinions on which origin of law(s) has more importance. This can lead to dissonance in educational settings. What occurs when one's perspective on divine law conflicts with that of a social contract? What happens when a social contract seems to diverge with natural law? What occurs when a perspective on natural law conflicts with that of divine law? Or, what occurs when one aspect of divine law seems to conflict with another aspect of divine law? In all these cases, the result is an ethical dilemma. An *ethical dilemma* is a circumstance where the right course(s) of action is(are) uncertain. Ethical dilemmas can result in tension between individuals in educational settings. These dilemmas occur regularly and pose some of the greatest challenges to college and university leaders.

DISCUSSION QUESTIONS

- What defines your moral compass? For example, what theories, models, beliefs, and assumptions comprise your compass? Where do these ideas and concepts come from?
- Consider the three perspectives on the origins of law (e.g., divine, natural, and social). How could these perspectives influence whether one views the law as a fixed ethical standard or fluid agreement?

DEFINITIONS

Divine law: suggests that laws originate from a divine source (e.g., God, supernatural deity).

Ethicians: scholars of ethics and morality

Ethics: the systematic, critical, and summative study of standards needed for moral living.

Ethical dilemma: a circumstance where the right course(s) of action is uncertain.

Ethical leadership: the practice of inspiring others towards a desired outcome while exemplifying an established standard for moral living.

Leadership: influencing and inspiring others beyond desired outcomes.

Moral compass: a personal framework of rules, principles, and virtues that guide one's actions, beliefs, and decision-making.

Morality: adhering to one's ethical standards through thoughts and behaviors.

Natural law: the perspective that rules and laws originate from nature; the *natural* or inherent drive for the human race to continue and thrive.

Self-awareness: one's knowledge of one's own assumptions, dispositions, values, and mores as it relates to what is, and is not, ethical.

Social contract: the perspective that laws originate from the societal level through individual's who give up their certain innate laws to the state, in exchange for a social order.

CHAPTER 3

COMMUNITY COLLEGE LEADERS' MORAL OBLIGATIONS

This chapter begins with a discussion of ethical breaches that have negatively impacted community colleges. It starts with an articulation of how small ethical violations can accumulate to large-scale violations as a result of contentment. The moral and civic inter-intrapersonal and structural responsibilities of community college leaders are then explored. This chapter concludes with a discussion of the community college mission and examines leaders' duty to its advancement.

When reading this chapter, consider the following questions:

- What ethical quandaries have you experienced as an educational leader?
- What are the conditions necessary for small ethical violations to become larger ones?
- What are the moral inter/intrapersonal responsibilities of college leaders?
- What are the moral structural responsibilities of college leaders?
- What is the mission of the community college? What (if any) are the moral duties that leaders have to this mission?

Ethical Leadership and the Community College: Paradigms, Decision-Making, and Praxis,
pages 23–36.
Copyright © 2014 by Information Age Publishing
All rights of reproduction in any form reserved.

The importance of ethical leadership in community colleges cannot be understated. However, "due to the increasingly complex nature of leadership, long work hours, high levels of stress, elevated expectations, and slow-moving bureaucracies, leaders are challenged to make 'right,' and often difficult, decisions on a daily basis" (Nevarez & Wood, 2010, p. 100). Leaders are expected to exercise properly their responsibility (Vaughan, 1992).

There are numerous examples of leaders in religion (e.g., Jim Jones, Warren Jeffs, and Jim Bakker), business (Bernie Madoff, Kenneth Lay, and Allen Stanford), and politics (e.g., Mark Sanford, Eliot Spitzer, William Jefferson, Jack Abramoff, and John Ensign) who have fallen short of their ethical responsibilities. These leaders did not possess or, at the very least, ignored their moral compass. Almost invariably, they were blinded by the pursuit of money, power, and glory. As a result their actions, as well as actions by numerous other leaders not mentioned here, public scrutiny for all leaders has been elevated. This is inclusive of college leaders.

THE INFLUENCE OF UNETHICAL ENVIRONMENTS

Over the past decade, multiple two-year college institutions have also experienced large breeches of ethical conduct. Ethical breeches serve to impact negatively all parties involved, students, faculty, staff, campus administration, the local community, and even other institutions of higher education. Consider the following examples:

- Diablo Valley College is a community college in California with a stellar educational reputation; however, it came under tense state and national scrutiny for a grade-changing scandal. Between the years 2000 and 2006, nearly 400 grades were changed in the admissions office by campus employees. Grades were changed by student record officials in exchange for cash payment and, in some cases, sexual favors. As the police investigation progressed, it was found that students from a sister campus in the same district (Los Medanos College in Pittsburg) also participated in the grade changing scandal. In all, 53 students from Diablo Valley and Los Medanos were charged in the case (Krupnick, 2007, 2008; Lee, 2007; Mytelka, 2007).
- Barton County Community College in Kansas (now Barton Community College) had a large athletic scandal which saw the convictions of their athletic director and seven coaches. Prison time was served by four individuals in all. A federal investigation found mail, wire, and financial fraudulency's, including: falsely seeking a medical hardship from the National Junior College Athletic Association for a basketball player in order to increase his eligibility; using federal work-study and campus employment to circumvent athletic scholarship rules; sending incorrect academic records to university officials on behalf of student athletes; preparing false time

sheets to increase pay for student athletes; and ordering an assistant coach to pose as a student to take an online course (Associated Press, 2006).

• The community college system in Alabama came under fire for allegations of criminal misconduct. A lengthy federal investigation uncovered a culture of illegal actions that resulted in guilty pleas and convictions of fifteen people including state representatives, a college chancellor, college presidents, a president's wife, a dean, and many others. They were either charged or convicted of crimes ranging from bribery, theft, conspiracy, obstruction of justice, kickbacks, cover-ups, falsely collecting pay, mail fraud, and money laundering. Administrators affiliated with Shelton State Community College, Gadsden State Community College, and Southern Union Community College were implicated in the case (Beyerle, 2009; Taylor, 2010).

These three examples serve to illustrate how a 'culture of unethical behavior' can lead to widespread corruption. When a 'culture of unethical behavior' exists, what would normally be viewed as clearly 'right' or 'wrong,' can appear to be grey. The truth is, being an ethical leader is a difficult task. So often, it is not the large blunders that affect a leader's success. It is not embezzlement, sexual scandal, accreditation fraudulency, or some other horrible act committed by a small minority of educational leaders. It is the minor questionable acts of behavior occurring over time that ultimately create an unethical culture, thereby allowing egregious ethical quandaries to occur. When unethical environments are left unchecked via a lack of accountability, a continuous toxic culture of immoral practices becomes commonplace. In other words, when unethical behavior is overlooked, it becomes the norm. This established climate pressures individuals to engage in unethical practices to be part of the 'in-group.' In many cases, would-be ethical leaders violate their moral inclinations to survive and protect their careers. Balancing the interests of familial responsibilities, income, and career vitality with the realities of institutional culture can challenge one's ethical standards. Ultimately, inculcating oneself in the established mores of such an environment may be beneficial in the short term, but eventually, either through new (external) leadership, state oversight, accreditation reviews, legislative mandates, judicial intervention, or other mechanisms, accountability will follow. This leads to a climate of unprincipled behavior that pressures moral leaders to sacrifice their ethical standards. This ultimately 'catches up' with community college leaders. For example, in all of the cases above, the campus president was either fired or forced to resign, thus the implications for ethical leadership throughout a college is clear.

THE PITFALLS OF CONTENTMENT

Unethical behavior can begin with small ethical breaches (i.e., a "white lie," an omission of truth, an unclear insinuation, false flattery, hiding behind the veil of duty, or avoiding responsibility). These behaviors can lead to contentment, where leaders begin to violate their personal moral compass, little by little, day by day.

When this occurs, each time one's moral compass is violated, the violation can become a little less bothersome. Over time, the notion of operating in gray (as opposed to black or white) can become more tolerable. Sometimes, leaders do not even realize that they are operating in this fashion. When this occurs, a seemingly minor action here and there becomes a little more endurable and somewhat less repulsive, and then, it can become practice. Ultimately, these subtle ethical violations serve to taint leaders' reputations. They serve to allow leadership to drift off course. As time progresses, this can result in leaders ending up in a place far away from where they expected. Major ethical breeches can be avoided through an administration that fosters transparency and accountability. As ambassadors of their institutions, community college leaders need to have the reflection needed to develop their personal moral compass, the fortitude to use it, the insight to recognize when they are off course, and the integrity to regain course when needed. However, over time, leaders who do not employ their moral compasses will reap the detriment of their actions. As the old adage goes, "what happens in the dark comes to the light."

ETHICAL LEADERSHIP RESPONSIBILITY

Community and university leaders should consider the following question, "why should I be an ethical leader?" We suggest, that with leadership comes not only greater power, money and prestige, but more importantly, greater responsibility. Many college employees know of leaders who have been bestowed the privilege of great responsibility, but have fallen short of the mark (Vaughan, 1992). In fact, it may be easier (in some cases) to identify individuals who are viewed as being unethical rather than those who are perceived as being ethical. As a result, when a leader is referred to as 'ethical' by their colleagues, followers, and peers, it is one of the greatest honors they can receive. When someone is called an 'ethical leader,' 'moral leader,' or 'righteous person,' it carries with it a significant symbolic worth.

College leaders have responsibilities to multiple individuals and entities, this includes: students, faculty members, staff/administrative team, the local community, the profession, governing boards, feeder institutions, other postsecondary educational institutions, and (of course) to themselves. Leaders should understand that failing to meet the multitude of responsibilities they have in these areas can be unethical. According to Starratt (2004), when leaders take office, they assume *ex-ante* responsibilities. *Ex-ante responsibilities* are expectations of office which leaders voluntarily assume by nature of the positions they acquire. These responsibilities are known, either by being explicitly stated in their contracts or by common knowledge, before the leader ever takes office. Thus, when leaders do not fulfill these responsibilities, they are violating a common-sense, and sometimes written, agreement between themselves and the institutions that they lead. Given the importance of these *ex–ante* responsibilities, we explicate *some* of the numerous areas in which they are evident.

Students

College leaders have an *ex-ante* responsibility to the students that they serve. They are responsible to:

a. provide them with a safe learning environment;
b. create a supportive atmosphere where student learning is of paramount concern;
c. establish high expectations for academic performance;
d. supply ample academic and social support services that aid student performance;
e. ensure quality teaching and learning is occurring in the classroom;
f. provide for a holistic learning environment where students' affective, cognitive, moral development is taking place;
g. maintain clear communication between students and the institution;
h. ensure that proper alignment within university channels of communication is occurring; and
i. establish course offerings allowing students to meet their educational and career goals.

Faculty members

Leaders in the community college also assume *ex-ante* responsibilities for faculty members. These responsibilities include:

a. dignified treatment of faculty as important agents in the education of students;
b. equitable treatment in hiring, promotion, tenure, and merit processes;
c. supporting an environment of creativity and academic freedom;
d. providing faculty with ample technological and classroom resources to instruct students effectively;
e. including faculty as important and integral components of campus decision-making;
f. ensuring fair salaries for faculty across racial/ethnic, gender, and disciplinary affiliations;
g. managing student load distributions to provide for workplace equity;
h. respecting the integrity of diverse pedagogical practices; and
i. listening and responding to faculty concerns in a timely and considerate manner.

Staff /Administrative Team

College leaders should also recognize the responsibilities they have to their staff members. These *ex-ante* responsibilities for college leaders include:

a. maintaining an environment of affirmation and support for staff members;
b. providing staff members with accurate and timely information;
c. ensuring fair treatment in the performance evaluation process;
d. recognizing staff members' contributions to organizational success;
e. including staff members in the decision-making process;
f. allowing staff a 'safe space' to make decisions without micro-management;
g. encouraging staff members to participate in professional development trainings;
h. providing a platform to address staff members concerns; and
i. ensuring equitable workload distribution among staff members.

Local Community

As leaders of community-centered institutions, college leaders have numerous *ex-ante* responsibilities to their local communities. Among the most important of these responsibilities are:

a. supplying programs responding to the economic needs of the community;
b. ensuring graduates are adequately educated to meet workforce needs;
c. ensuring healthy college-community partnerships are established and maintained;
d. serving as a socio-cultural center for community activities;
e. providing service-learning and civic engagement opportunities benefitting the local community;
f. ensuring individuals in the local community have access to the institution and its resources (e.g., library); and
g. providing transportation opportunities, extension sites, off-site learning, and online learning opportunities which expand admission to all communities within its service region.

The Profession

College leaders have several important responsibilities to the profession. As 'professionals' and ambassadors of the greater community college, leadership should:

a. adhere to all ethical codes of conduct as articled by the American Association of Community Colleges (AACC)[1], and other ethical codes as established at the state, district, and local level;

---

[1] See AACC's *Recommended Code of Ethics for CEOs of Community Colleges*

b.   be up to date on recent research (e.g., pedagogy, andragogy, and leadership) that can serve to enhance their practice of leadership and the faculty, staff, students, and local communities they serve;

c.   maintain constant and critical discussions with colleagues on effective
leadership and learning practices;

d.   uphold the five-fold mission of the community college (explicated further in the next section); and

e.   avoid behavior and practices which would place a negative light on community colleges and their leaders.

Governing Board

Leaders of community colleges have multiple responsibilities to their oversight boards. These responsibilities include:

a.   providing boards with accurate and timely information;

b.   implementing board-mandated policies and procedures;

c.   guiding board actions with the intention of benefiting the institutions that
they serve; this is inclusive of providing respectful but critical feedback
on intended and enacted decisions;

d.   creating an environment of professional collaboration and mutual respect;

e.   accurately communicating board decisions to organizational subordi-
nates; and

f.   assuming responsibility for organizational successes and failures.

Feeder Institutions

Feeder institutions (e.g., adult learning centers, high schools, or community
centers) are vital to the success of community colleges. Thus, community college
leaders have several important responsibilities to these institutions, they include:

a.   easing students' transition from the feeder institution to college through
the application, assessment, advising and enrollment processes;

b.   ensuring accurate, clear, timely, and effective communication occurs between community college officials and feeder institution officials; and

c.   providing ample resources and services to ensure feeder institution students' academic and social needs are met.

Postsecondary Institutions

Many students transition between community colleges and some from community colleges to four year institutions. As a result, community college leaders
have several primary responsibilities to other postsecondary educational institutions, these include:

a.   providing accurate and timely student records;

b.   ensuring that passing grades are given *only* in courses in which students illustrate a thorough knowledge of the content taught; and

c.   implementing procedures which ensure students have taken a proper sequence of coursework.

Themselves

While leaders have important responsibilities to multiple constituencies and entities, they also have responsibilities to themselves. They have a responsibility to implement professional decisions they can 'live with;' decisions that do not violate their personal moral compass. This may require leaders to withdraw themselves from taking certain actions and/or in extreme circumstances, to resign their posts. Leaders also have a responsibility to maintain a level of balance between their personal lives and professional lives. This balance requires leaders to ensure that their personal and familial needs (e.g., physical, financial, psychological, spiritual, and social) have been met. This point is described further in Chapter 10, titled The Ethic of Care.

The *ex-ante* responsibilities articulated in this section serve as a baseline for understanding the expected roles of community college leaders. However, in and of themselves, they merely maintain the status quo and do not necessarily advocate transformation. The authors of this volume assert that ethical leadership is embodied within a transformative leadership approach. Transformative leadership "is a social justice-oriented approach undergirded by notions of democracy (e.g., opportunity, equity, fairness, freedom). Leaders using this framework seek to identify, challenge, and redress issues of marginalization, power, privilege, and subjugation in society" (Nevarez, Wood, & Penrose, 2013, p. 143). The challenges facing community colleges today require leaders who see problems in the ways that institutions have operated in the past and advocate for new directions that create better opportunities and outcomes for students and the communities they serve. Too often, problems with community colleges (e.g., dismal outcomes for men of color, inadequate services for immigrant students, limited advising, and counseling support) are overlooked as they require time, energy, and resources that are not part of the institution's "top" priorities. Transformative leaders value change, realizing that their commitment to the public good is not to a select few, but to the greater public, and even those on the 'margins' of the institution. This notion is spirited in the expansive mission of the community college. Figure 3.1 depicts the ethical responsibilities articulated in this section, beginning with transformative leadership as a starting point. Transformative leadership is associated with many core virtues, including: transformation, change, advocacy, equity, diversity, and social justice.

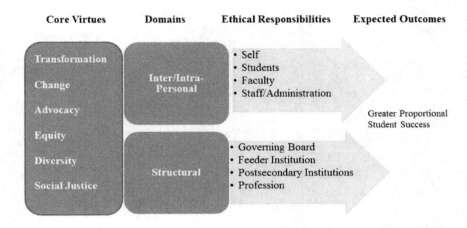

Core Virtues	Domains	Ethical Responsibilities	Expected Outcomes

FIGURE 3.1. Valued Duties of Ethical Leaders.

DUTY TO THE COMMUNITY COLLEGE MISSION

In addition to the previously describe responsibilities, community college leaders also have an important set of cardinal duties to uphold. We delineate between responsibilities in duties in that the *duties* are highly esteemed or valued responsibilities. Duties have a greater level of importance in comparison to responsibilities, though both are often used interchangeably and connote an ethical underpinning. It is the duty of community college leaders to uphold the six-fold mission of the community college. To do so, is to maintain the ethical principles of equity, diversity, opportunity, and local community for which the community college is known.

Prominent community college scholar George Vaughan describes five core components of the institutions mission, this includes: open access, comprehensive educational programs, serving the community, teaching and learning, and lifelong learning (Vaughan, 2006). Nevarez and Wood (2010) provided one additional mission component: student success. These components and their ethical implications are addressed below. Much of the ethical issues raised in context of the community college mission relate to the ethic of local community (serving the best interests and needs of the local community), and ethic of critique (advocating for the rights and bests interests of the underserved). Figure 3.2 presents the relationship between the mission components of the community college and the primary ethical paradigms with which they *tend* to intersect.

Open access refers to community colleges' commitment to provide educational opportunities for all students who desire a postsecondary education. This commitment has resulted in open-door policies that allow *nearly* any person interested in attending these institutions to do so. As a result, students enrolling in the com-

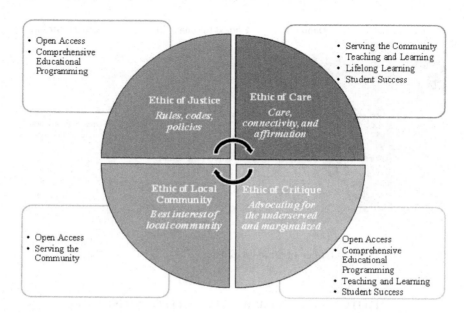

FIGURE 3.2. Relationship between Mission Components and Ethical Paradigms

munity college illustrate a wide array of diverse affiliations (e.g., racial/ethnic, gender, age, socioeconomic, national origin, and religious belief). Open access has allowed community colleges to serve students that would, in many cases, not be served by public/private four-year institutions. Further, Vaughan (2006) notes that the principle of open access is rooted in democratic ideas, asserting that the nation's survival relies upon the country's ability to provide educational opportunities to the masses. Given the prominence of open access, its importance as an ethical ideal to the community college should be understood by current and aspiring college leaders. Simply stated, open-access is the ethical fiber of the community college. Thus, ensuring the maintenance and continuation of this policy should be an ethical concern for community college leaders.

Comprehensive educational programming is the community colleges' commitment to ensuring a wide range of academic programming (e.g., remediation, vocational-technical education, continuing education, terminal degrees, and preparation for transfer) is provided. Vaughan (2006) noted that a diversity of academic programming is needed for community colleges to fill a multiplicity of local community needs. While providing preparation to transfer from two to four-year institutions remains a core component of the educational programming provided, community colleges have responded to varied educational/career goals that their students' maintain. This core mission component has provided the community college with the opportunity of serving adult returnees, senior citizens, high school students, and working parents. In more recent years, the community college's commitment to comprehensive educational programming has expanded its purview to include the offering of baccalaureate degrees. In general, this occurs in two primary ways: 1) community colleges offer stand-alone baccalaureate programs; and 2) community colleges offer baccalaureate programs with partners from public/private universities. Baccalaureate degree offerings are focused on meeting workforce demands. In particular, they are concentrated in the fields of education, health, business, and law enforcement. Providing an array of educational programming is an important ethical consideration for community college leaders. Doing so ensures that the institution is providing educational opportunities that students' would likely not be able to receive otherwise. However, providing broad academic programming can also be burdensome. Such programming can result in having excessive foci in too many areas, which can result in mediocre academic offerings. Avoiding this pitfall is also an ethical concern for community college leaders as it can lead to poor quality in all areas. Thus, community college leaders should be mindful of the need to provide widespread programming, but should consider emphasizing their efforts in one or two areas. This will allow community colleges to provide varied programming while maintaining academic integrity and quality with these offerings.[2]

Serving the community refers to the community colleges core mission of serving the local community. Placing the local community first is a unique responsibility for community colleges in that it is a mission-related mandate that many other postsecondary institutions do not share. In order to serve local community needs, community college leaders' must have an understanding of impending local issues (e.g., economic, socio-cultural, and educational) and trends as well as a clear knowledge of current issues. With an understanding of impending and current issues, community college leaders are charged with implementing preventions and interventions that address local community needs. Given the widespread nature of possible local needs, priority should be given to issues which can be resolved through the expansion and/or revision of academic programming. Three examples serve to illustrate this point:

1. college leaders who have service areas that are too far from the central campus to have high levels of college-going can create extension centers to provide additional access for students;

2. institutions imbedded in communities with wide-ranging social issues (e.g., homelessness, healthcare access, and nutrition) can engage in service-learning activities with partner organizations addressing these issues; and

3. community colleges recognizing that high school students from feeder schools are not adequately prepared for college may begin offering col-

---

[2] In layman's terms, this means community colleges should be "a jack of all trades, master of one" not a "jack of all trades, master of none."

legiate preparatory courses for aspiring collegians. Serving the community is a core ethical imperative for community colleges. This mission embodies the spirit of the institution in being a community-focused educational institution. In essence, this mission component signifies leaders' need to focus on the 'community' in 'community college.'

Teaching and learning refers to the community colleges' mission of providing high quality instruction in academic and professional disciplines from which students can learn practical and theoretical knowledge. Further, this mission also suggests that the knowledge learned can be applied in 'real world' settings. Teaching and learning occurs in community colleges in two primary domains. Firstly, the institution is committed to students' cognitive development; this "accounts for the ways an individual develops critical thinking and reasoning processes" (Barr et al., 2000, p. 236). Secondly, community colleges also educate students with the purpose of enhancing their affective development; this "involves the temperamental, emotional, self-esteem, and self-concept development of individuals" (Nevarez & Wood, 2010, p. 182). The teaching and learning mission of the community college originates from the early conception of the community college as a pre-university institution where students could complete their general education coursework before entering higher levels of study. This notion of the community college as an institution dedicated to teaching and learning is still evident. This mission component can be juxtaposed with the mission of many four-year universities which are geared toward research and discovery. As noted by Nevarez and Wood (2010), this mission component "is not necessarily one of generating new knowledge (e.g., research), but providing access to knowledge (e.g., practical teaching and learning) for communities from which it has been elusive" (p. 7). While the community colleges history of educating diverse populations (e.g., students of color, older students, part-time students, and low-income students) is not without its blemishes, it has done exceedingly well in this regard since the 1960s. Community colleges have provided opportunities for underserved communities to attain higher levels of academic knowledge. Essentially, it has succeeded where the ivory tower (e.g., elite universities) have fallen short. Thus, providing quality instruction and ensuring that learning is transpiring is a foundational ethical necessity for community college leaders. In reality, this mission component is shared by many public teaching universities and private liberal arts college. However, when considered in tandem with the community colleges' mission of open access, the importance of teaching and learning signifies the institutions unique role of providing knowledge to the masses.

Lifelong learning indicates the community colleges' commitment to the educational development of students' throughout their life spans. Vaughan (2006) notes the importance of this mission component. He suggests a traditional approach to educating students has focused on providing educational learning for a contained period of time. Under this model, when students have graduated they would likely never continue their education, unless under the pursuit of a more advanced degree. Rapid changes in technology, management techniques, and disciplinary knowledge have shown this model to be an outdated approach. As a result, the community college continues to serve students throughout their life spans; viewing learning as a continual process. This occurs by providing professional development, general education, and leisure coursework and programming that allows students of all ages to continue learning. The importance of this mission component cannot be understated. The great recession emerging in the first decade of the 21st century forced a large portion of the workforce (and even many retirees) to return to college, and 'retool' their skills, knowledge, and competencies for new employment. This resulted in expansive enrollment for many community colleges. As with the mission components of comprehensive educational programming and serving the local community, lifelong learning coursework and programming should be focused in areas meeting local needs. Thus, attention should be given to academic programming addressing at least one of the following areas: a) the greatest local demand; b) a potential for the maximization institutional resources; and c) a probable influx of revenue. Like the other mission components, lifelong learning is an ethical element of the community college mission. Lifelong learning provides wide ranging educational opportunities for students. These opportunities are not as easily provided by many four-year institutions either due to the focus of their mission or the limitations of admissions requirements.

Student success refers to the community colleges' mission of aiding students in attaining their academic and career goals. Specifically, this mission component represents the institutions dedication to providing resources, services, and programming that support students in actualizing their goals. Providing educational opportunities to students has been a core value of community colleges since their inception. However, this value has been manifested from two distinct viewpoints. The first viewpoint suggests that access be provided to students; allowing each student the *right to fail*; hence, some students will rise to the expectations placed before them, while others will fail. However, as noted by Cohen and Brawer (2003) and Richardson (1987), this perspective has brought high levels of scrutiny to community colleges as institutions that do not have the ability to aid students in achieving their goals. The second viewpoint, as embodied by the mission component of student success, suggests that all students have a *right to succeed.* As a result, when students are admitted to the community college, the institution assumes a responsibility to support their success. As such, community colleges should provide support mechanisms seeking to create educational equity (e.g., enrollment, graduation, and transfer) and success (e.g., persistence and high GPAs) for diverse student groups (e.g., students of color, low income students, and older students) throughout their academic paths (e.g., remediation, general education, and vocational-technical education). Student success is a chief ethical principle which community college leaders should uphold. Despite the fact that reductions in state funding and increases in enrollment have strained resources at many institutions, leaders must remain dedicated to supporting student success. For many underserved communities, two-year colleges are the most likely pathway into a four-year university. The high numbers of students of color, adult returnees, and low-income students attending these institutions are a testament to the universal confidence in the community college to meet this end. Thus, dismal persistence, graduation, and transfer rates among specific subgroups should indicate a failure to the local community. They represent a violation of the institution's integrity and pose a serious ethical dilemma.

DISCUSSION QUESTIONS

1.   The slow progression from small ethical violations to larger ones was identified in this chapter (the pitfalls of contentment). Do you agree with this perspective? If so, how have you seen this play out in practice?
2.   Do you believe that community college leaders have a moral responsibility to the community college mission? If so, why? If not, why not?
3.   This chapter addressed a number of *ex-ante* responsibilities for community college leaders. What do you believe are the most essential of these responsibilities? What role do the standards of the professional have (if any) in ethical decision-making?

DEFINITIONS

Comprehensive educational programming: the community colleges' commitment to ensuring wide ranging academic programming (e.g., remediation, vocational-technical education, continuing education, terminal degrees, and preparation for transfer).

Duties: highly esteemed or valued responsibilities as they have a greater level of importance.

Ex-ante responsibilities: the expectations of office that leaders voluntarily assume by nature of the positions they acquire.

Lifelong learning: indicates the community colleges' commitment to the educational development of students' throughout their life spans.

Open access: refers to community colleges' commitment to provide educational opportunities for all students who desire a postsecondary education.

Serving the community: refers to the community colleges core mission of serving the local community.

Student success: refers to the community colleges' mission of aiding students in attaining their academic and career goals.

Teaching and learning: refers to the community colleges' mission of providing high-quality instruction in academic and professional disciplines from which students can learn practical and theoretical knowledge.

CHAPTER 4

POWER AND ETHICS IN COMMUNITY COLLEGE LEADERSHIP

This chapter begins with a discussion on the linkage between power and ethics, noting that power influences and intensifies leaders moral propensities. Then, power and its core dimensions (e.g., scope, domain, weight, cost) are defined and explored. Varying types of power are explored as informed by the works of John French, Bertam Raven, Gary Yukl, and Pierre Bourdieu. The chapter concludes by articulating the five principles (e.g., purpose, pride, patience, persistence, and perspective) of ethical decision-making as described by Blanchard and Peale.

When reading this chapter, consider the following questions:

- What is the relationship between power, leadership, and ethics?
- How is power defined? What are the primary dimensions of power?
- What are the primary types of personal and positional power? What is the effect of these forms of power on the decision-making process?
- What are the five principles of ethical decision-making?

Ethical Leadership and the Community College: Paradigms, Decision-Making, and Praxis,
pages 37–47.
Copyright © 2014 by Information Age Publishing

The sole advantage of power is that you can do more good.

> —*Baltasar Gracian*

Power, leadership, and ethics are concepts that are inextricably intertwined. Leadership is inherently typified by power relations between individuals, resources, strategic direction, and organizational decision-making. Those who have power have greater influence, and with greater influence come greater responsibility. In some ways, without situational, organizational, and personal power, ethics in organizational contexts is a less salient topic. Power can often lead to ethical quandaries. To address this relationship, organizational policies are often set in place to control power dynamics between leaders and followers. For example, policies regarding travel and reimbursements, nepotism, faculty-student relationships, and conflict of interest are often set in place to ensure those with positional power maintain a respectable level of integrity when carrying out the duties of their office. However, policy in and of itself cannot control power, nor account for the multiplicity of power intricacies and dynamics in bureaucratic settings.

It is often assumed that there is a unidirectional relationship between power and ethics, where power influences ethics, not the opposite. In fact, it is commonly perceived that power exposes the true ethical standards and moral actions of individuals by intensifying their core propensities. Numerous catchphrases and quotes illustrate the perceived relationships between power and ethics:

Nearly all men can stand adversity, but if you want to test a man's character, give him power.

> —*Abraham Lincoln*

The essence of government is power; and power, lodged as it must be in human hands, will ever be liable to abuse.

> —*James Madison*

The problem of power is how to achieve its responsible use rather than its irresponsible and indulgent use—of how to get men of power to live for the public rather than off the public.

> —*Robert F. Kennedy*

Power tends to corrupt, and absolute power corrupts absolutely.

> —*Lord Acton*

Fear of losing power corrupts those who wield it and fear of the scourge of power corrupts those who are subject to it.

> —*Aung San Suu Kyi*

Power in the hands of the reformer is no less potentially corrupting than in the hands of the oppressor.

—Derrick A. Bell

As evident within these quotes, power is often equated with a lack of ethics. Of course, in reality, this is not always the case; however, when used unwisely and without considerable thought, power *can* result in corruption. To ensure the proper use of power, leaders must first have an understanding of what power is, the dimensions it occurs in, and the many forms that it takes. Armed with this knowledge, they can be more proactive in properly executing the authority of their posts and holding others accountable to the same end.

POWER AND ITS DIMENSIONS

Power refers to the capacity to influence others through the use of authority. What this influence is used for often determines whether the execution of power is ethical or unethical. When used to advance organizational objectives, the community college mission, local community interests, and the general welfare of its personnel (e.g., faculty, staff, and administration) and students, power is often wielded ethically. However, when used to advance personal interest, vendettas, and to marginalize other powerbrokers, power is used immorally. Power is complex, as its use and manifestations are multidimensional in nature.

As articulated by Baldwin (2002), power occurs in several dimensions. These include (but are not limited to): scope, domain, weight, and cost. *Scope* refers to the facet of organizational life in which power takes place. In some organizational contexts, one individual holds a certain degree of power; however, in other contexts that person may have more limited power. For example, a director of enrollment management will have more power on committees that are influenced by his/her line of work than on committees less impacted by enrollment concerns. Primarily, scope of power is related to issues for which the actor using power has advanced knowledge, skills, and experience. *Domain* refers to the structural residence of power within the organizational structure. For instance, regardless of relevance to their line of work, an academic dean may hold extensive power on committees under their college's jurisdiction, but have more limited power on student service committees. While this is somewhat related to scope, the key point here is that organizations have structures, and knowledge within one domain (academic affairs) may not be respected in other domains (student affairs) and vice versa. *Weight* refers to the likelihood that the outcome will be a result of the actor's intentions. In other words, the actor with the greatest probability of achieving their intentions will have greater weight in decision-making than those who do not. For example, a leader who has the respect of their colleagues will often emerge victorious over leaders who are held in lower esteem among their peers. This can even occur when the un-respected leader's position is more convincing and their organizational authority is greater than that of the leader with the most 'weight.' *Cost* refers to the expense of resources and capital in achieving a desired end. A leader who can achieve their intended outcome with limited expenditure of political capital is more powerful than the leader who must place their capital on the line to achieve their goal. Power can be held by individuals, sometimes irrespective of title and post. The next section explores this notion further.

LEADERSHIP AND POWER

As noted earlier, with leadership comes greater power. This is true for both formal and informal leaders. *Formal leaders* are individuals who possess positions of authority. This is inclusive of the following posts: Chancellor, Superintendent, President, Vice President, Associate Vice President, Assistant Vice President, Dean, Associate Dean, Assistant Dean, Program Director, etc. *Informal leaders* are leaders who do not hold a formal position of authority, but through their influence are able to wield power in organizational decision-making processes. For example, a senior faculty member may not hold a formal position within the organizational structure of an institution; however, they may be able to influence a large number of faculty, staff, and/or students to support or oppose institutional mandates, policies, and procedures. This influence is derived through peer respect, trust, credibility, work ethic, and commitment to advancing virtues and values of interest to the greater good.

Power is an important ethical topic, especially the manner in which it is used. Power is an ethical issue for two reasons: 1) whenever one individual has power over another, there is a potential for misuse and abuse; and 2) power brings with it a responsibility to provide for the welfare of those who hold lesser power. In and of itself, power is neither a virtue nor a vice. The manner in which power is wielded by its holder(s) determines its nature. Understanding power and the various forms in which it occurs is important for community college leaders. This understanding will enable leaders to forecast and avoid potential areas in which ethical pitfalls can occur.

Power occurs in two primary domains, the first is an individual's personal power (irrespective of their post within an institution); the second is power derived for one's position within an organization or use of its resources. Power can be conceptualized in many forms. In this text, we focus on power as explicated by:

a.   John French and Bertam Raven's (1959) five forms of power;
b.   Gary Yukl's (1994) critique of French and Raven's work; and
c.   Pierre Bourdieu's (2001) forms of capital.

With respect to the latter, capital is viewed as akin to power in that it advantages one group/individual over other groups/individuals. Bourdieu (2001) identifies three primary forms of capital, cultural, social, capital, and resource capital. Bourdieu (2001) stated that "*cultural capital*...may be institutionalized in the form of educational qualifications; and as *social capital*, [is] made up of social obligations (connections)" (p. 98). Bourdieu (1997, 2001) stated that economic capital can exist as money or objects that are transferrable into money (such as equipment, property ownership, livestock).

Personal Power

Cultural capital is knowledge that is possessed by an individual, particularly knowledge gained through socialization, exposure to objects, and academic pursuits. It is the capital of knowing what to do, when to do it, and why to do it. Thus, this form of capital is primarily cognitive in nature. Cultural capital exists in three primary forms:

• embodied state;
• objectified state; and
• institutionalized state.

The *embodied state* is capital that is attained primary through familial relations and socialization. *Objectified state* is related to economic capital in that it exists in objects (e.g., art, books, and machinery) which are owned. As such, the resulting knowledge and understanding that comes from exposure to these objects is a form of cultural capital.

Institutionalized state refers to educational credentials (e.g., degrees, certificates, etc.) that symbolize and recognize the acquisition of knowledge (Bourdieu, 2001, 2003; Bourdieu & Wacquant, 1992; Calhoun, Gerteis, Moody, Pfaff, & Virk, 2002; Grenfell et al., 1998). In college administration, cultural capital in the institutionalized state (e.g., educational credentials) is of particular importance. Higher levels of education: provide increased career mobility, increased social and professional networks, enhanced job skills, enhanced earning potential, and most importantly, enhanced professional credibility (Futrell, 1999; Levinson, 2007; Nevarez & Wood, 2010; Vernez & Mizell, 2001).

There are multiple types of cultural capital; however, one important form is linguistic capital. *Linguistic capital* is "class-linked traits of speech differentially valued in a specific field or marked" (Collins, 1993, p. 118). According to Bourdieu and Passeron (1990), the effect of linguistic capital is most easily seen in the earlier educational levels. Language style and dialect are often taken into account in teacher's assessments of students' ability. These judgments continue throughout the educational system, into higher education, and inevitably, into the administrative ranks in organizations (i.e., the community college). A leader with linguistic capital is perceived as possessing more than intellect, but the culturally appropriate method of communicating in a professional language style and dialect.

French and Raven (1959) present a form of personal power that is akin to Bourdieu's (2001) notion of cultural capital; it is referred to as expert power. *Expert power* is power derived from an individual's possession of expert knowledge that can be used to address dilemmas and undertake certain tasks. Yukl (1994) noted that expert power (or expertise) is enhanced when followers have difficulty in locating other dependable sources of knowledge. He suggests that, in some cases, a leader's perceived knowledge of policies, procedures, and appropriate actions is more important than the actual possession of that knowledge. More simply stated, perception is more important than reality. However, Yukl notes that as time progresses, a lack of expert power will become evident by followers. In some circumstances, leaders will initiate pre-planned crises in order to illustrate their expertise in resolving the crises. In order to maintain expert power, some leaders will employ (or create) high-level jargon to illustrate their intelligence and understanding. Many community college leaders use this approach, which is likely a result of the discourse community (e.g., educational leadership) to which they belong.

Social capital refers to capital or power attained through relationships; it is another primary form of capital proffered by Bourdieu. As noted by Bourdieu (2001), "it is the aggregate of the actual or potential resources that are linked to possession of a durable network of more or less institutionalized relationships" (pp. 102–103). Essentially, social capital focuses on the usage of networks to attain resources and other forms of capital within any given field (Bourdieu, 2005). Thus, the strength of social capital is based upon the power of those in which the relationships are held (Bourdieu, 1988). Raven & French (1959) offer a similar form of power, referred to as referent power. *Referent power* occurs when individuals' opinions are valued as a result of their personal character and qualities. In a slightly different conception, Yukl (1994) presents referent power as *friendship or loyalty*. He notes that followers are willing to carry out tasks for leaders when there is a sense of loyalty to the leader. As a result, Yukl notes that leaders can use symbolic acts of humility (e.g., pitching in on 'the dirty work') to illustrate that they are a member of the team; this is done to minimize the perception of evident differences between leaders and followers.

Another form of capital identified by Bourdieu is symbolic capital. *Symbolic capital* is capital related to prestige, respect and admiration. It is "the power granted to those who have obtained sufficient recognition to be in a position to impose recognition" (Bourdieu, 1990, p. 138). Symbolic capital can also be displayed through possessions symbolizing an individual's societal stature. In effect, symbolic capital focuses on the value and usefulness of one's popularity or reputation in a given society (Bourdieu, 1990, 1997; Bourdieu & Wacquant, 1992). Higher ranks of academic administration bring with it higher levels of symbolic capital. This capital is especially developed when leaders have a reputation for being effective at their craft (i.e., a college president known for making fiscally unstable institutions into stable institutions; a vice president well regarded for his/her ability to raise substantial funds from prospective donors).

Yukl (1994) also presents charisma as a variant of referent power (social capital). *Charisma* is a leader's ability to inspire others towards some action or goal based upon their charm. Leaders who employ charisma are often seen as holders of power, role models, or important figures. Charismatic leaders maintain a high degree of likeability among those whom they lead; this likeability can be associated with personal characteristics with which followers' desire. In many instances, followers desire recognition, approval, and favor from charismatic leaders. Informal and formal community college leaders can use charisma to wield substantial power within their respective institutions. It should be noted that charisma is easily used for both 'righteous' and 'immoral' practices.

Positional Power

Legitimate authority is a concept proffered by Raven & French (1959) suggesting that a leaders' position is a form of power. Thus, the mere position or title held by a leader can be accompanied with power. In some ways, this power is temporary and fluid, in that it is often associated with a post as opposed to a person. As such, when a leader leaves their post, except through a positional promotion, the power held by that leader dissipates. Yukl (1994) noted that legitimate power, which he refers to as formal authority, is evident when three important factors are present:

1.   followers maintain an internal value that respects the authority of a certain post and the leaders who assume those posts;
2.   followers identify with an organization/entity and are committed to its continuation and success; and
3.   followers are willing to adhere to the rules set forth by formal leaders in return for membership within an organization/entity.

Yukl notes that leaders who are selected through means perceived as illegitimate will suffer from lower levels of commitment to the aforementioned factors which can serve to derail their leadership agendas. For example, some community college leaders engage in special hires that allow them to circumvent conventional equal opportunity hiring practices. When this occurs, the authority of the special hire may not be valued, as followers within the organization can view them as an illegitimate member of an institution's leadership team. Further, faculty members who are hand-selected by academic leaders (e.g., Deans, Department Chairs, Program Directors, etc.) and hired through a 'tainted' search process can be viewed as illegitimate.

Resource capital refers to intellectual, labor, physical, and economic resources controlled by a leader. Bourdieu (1997, 2001) stated that economic capital can exist as money or objects that are transferrable into money (such as equipment, property, livestock, etc.). In organizational contexts, economic capital is akin to resource capital as economic resources can be used for the advantage of the leader. By virtue of their posts, many legitimate authorities can possess resource capital. These resources are often used by leaders to ensure loyalty from their followers. While many leaders in posts which are viewed as holding legitimate authority

TABLE 4.1. Types of power

Power Type	Variants
Personal Power	
	Cultural Capital
	Social Capital
Positional Power	
	Legitimate Authority
	(Economic) Resource Capital

Note: This is not an exhaustive list of personal and positional forms of power.

reap the benefits of greater resources, this is not always the case. For example, some community colleges have appointed executive leaders (e.g., vice president of diversity, chief diversity officer, etc.) who have limited staff resources, minimal budgets, and little decision-making authority. If/when their lack of resource capital becomes known, the quality of their legitimate authority and influence is likely weakened.

Raven and French (1959) identify two forms of resource capital, reward power and coercive power. Reward power refers to the ability of leaders to use their resource capital to benefit or advantage one or more employees. *Reward power* can be used to give loyal adherents: a promotion, pay increases, better schedules, enhanced budgets, greater levels of responsibility, increased authority, organizational recognition, larger or better located office space, and parking perks (Yukl, 1994). All this is distributed to ensure that there is optimal loyalty to the leader. *Coercive power* is the usage of resource capital to withhold rewards or intentionally punish followers who have not satisfied a formal authority. Yukl (1994) suggests that employee dismissal is not widely used as a form of coercive power. Due to the highly bureaucratic nature of community colleges, this may be true. Unfortunately, the use of resource capital to marginalize, alienate, and psychologically harm employees is used in lieu of dismissals to force employees to leave on their own volition. Yukl cautions leaders that the use of coercive power is only effective when applied to a limited group of followers under, what is perceived as, legitimate circumstances. Otherwise, leaders who use excessive coercion can be undermined by followers.

Control over information is another form of power used within organizations. Yukl (1994) notes that leaders who maintain power over information channels from superiors, outside entities, and other important sources can then construe the meaning of the information for employees. Thus, control over information can be used to guide followers understanding, perceptions, and feelings towards the information provided. Further, the information can be presented in part or in whole in a manner benefitting the intentions of the leader. When other information channels do not exist, control over the flow of information can become an important aspect of positional power. In some cases, leaders will release different pieces of information to different individuals in confidence, whom they know will not keep the information confidential, to paint a picture to followers which ensures their advantage. Followers can become powerful, even more powerful than their immediate legitimate authority, by gaining access to reliable information channels. As evident within all the aforementioned forms of power, ethical considerations are clear and compelling.

NEXT STEPS: FIVE PRINCIPLES

Blanchard and Peale (1988) developed five principles of ethical decision-making. These principles are used to ensure that power and influence are used in the right way. The five principles include purpose, pride, patience, persistence, and perspective. These principles can serve as a foundation for a leader's decision-making. In essence, leaders should consider these five principles when faced with ethical dilemmas to determine whether their course of action is appropriate and ethical. *Moral purpose* refers to a solidified sense of focus underscored by virtues/values of ethical behavior that serve as a filter for evaluating one's choices and decisions. This makes allowance for ethical behavior and allows individuals to "stay the course." Simply put, the authors of this volume believe that every person (and every leader) has a purpose in their life that is informed by ethical values. Thus, when making decisions, those decisions should be in line with and advance that purpose. *Moral pride* entails having a balanced sense of self-esteem connoting feelings of competence, confidence, self-worth, and pride. An unassuming disposition propels leaders to use power and influence in the right way. Individuals with an imbalanced sense of pride, who seek the acceptance and approval of others, may use power and influence for individual purposes and not to advocate for the greater good. A healthy sense of pride can foster ethical decision-making, while an overabundance of lack of pride can lead to deleterious effects. Leaders must be centered in balancing the line between humility and arrogance, making decisions that are reflective of a mean between these two points. *Moral patience* refers to functioning and living in a society rampant with the notion of the "here and now" can deter leaders from having the patience to follow ethical principles that advocate the right of conduct. This notion of immediate gratification as opposed to postponing gratification often leads advancing decisions not necessarily aligned with ethical principles and values. Having the patience and vetting decisions through a set of ethical values and virtues can underscore the positive aspect of ethical power. Patience entails not being too quick to arrive at a decision, but taking the time needed to vet decisions through different perspectives. The vetting process includes filtering decisions through ethical values. Too often, novice leaders make the mistake of rushing to decision-making. Having patience ensures that all appropriate considerations are vetted. This approach is easier said than done in a society where immediacy is the rule. *Moral persistence* entails insistency in the use of ethical principles to drive decision-making and allows for individuals to use power and influence for the right purpose. Vetting ethical dilemmas and matters through the use of a set of ethical values while showing unrelenting conviction to 'staying the course' serves as an additional aspect of the right use of power and influence. Finally, *moral perspective* involves the ability to contextualize and perceive situations in their relational importance to ethical values and virtues. It is about having an ability to perceive matters from both a micro- and macro-perspective and using this skill to guide decisions. It connotes moving away from making impulsive decisions and having the perspective to anticipate a multiplicity of views and approaches that will derive at sound ethical decision making. The subsequent chapters provide an overview of several paradigms that should inform leaders perspectives when engaged in decision-making. These paradigms include the ethic of justice, ethic of critique, ethic of care, and ethic of local community. Taken together, decision-making can (and should) be filtered through these perspectives to arrive at decisions which are sound, meaningful, deliberate, and impactful. In doing so, leaders will be able to better advance the community college mission.

DISCUSSION QUESTIONS

- As noted in the chapter, a widely held perspective is that power and ethics are inextricably linked. Do you believe this perspective to be accurate? If so, why? If not, why not?
- Different variants of personal and positional power were covered in this chapter (e.g., cultural capital, social capital, legitimate authority, resource capital, etc.). Provide two examples of the ethical dilemmas you have seen or experienced.

DEFINITIONS

Cost: refers to the expense of resources and capital in achieving a desired end.

Cultural capital: knowledge possessed by an individual, particularly knowledge gained through socialization, exposure to objects, and academic pursuits.

Domain: refers to the structural residence of power within the organizational structure.

Formal leaders: individuals who possess positions of authority within a community college.

Informal leaders: are leaders who do not hold a formal position of authority, but through their influence are able to wield power in organizational decision-making processes.

Legitimate authority: the notion that a leader's position is a form of power.

Moral patience: refers to patiently mai
   ing moral actions in a s
   "here and now."

Moral persistence: entails insistency i
   decision-making allowin
   fluence for the right purp

Moral perspective: entails involving th
   situations in their relatic
   virtues.

Moral pride: entails having a balance
   feelings of competence, (

Moral purpose: refers to a solidified s(
   values of ethical behavior that serves as a filter for evaluating
   one's choices and decisions.

Power: refers to the capacity to influence others through the use of authority.

Resource capital: the intellectual, labor, physical, and economic resources
   controlled by a leader.

Scope: refers to the facet of organizational life in which power takes place.

Social capital: refers to capital attained through relationships.

Weight: refers to the likelihood that the outcome will be a result of the actor's
   intentions.

PART II

FOUR ETHICAL DECISION-MAKING PARADGIMS

CHAPTER 5

THE ETHIC OF JUSTICE

This chapter, using examples from Plato's Republic, highlights some of the numerous definitions of justice. The authors discuss the varying types of justice (e.g., distributive and remedial), and articulate the Rawlsian perspective of justice. Guided by these theoretical underpinnings, the authors present the 'Ethic of Justice' as a decision-making framework guided by 'the rule of law' and the pursuit of a 'fair' society. The nuances and intricacies of this lens are discussed in context of leadership in the community college.

When reading this chapter, consider the following questions:

- What is justice? How is it defined?
- What are the competing notions of justice?
- What are the strengths and limitations of an ethic of justice approach?
- In what way (if any) can this framework enhance leadership and inform institutional change?

We begin this chapter by addressing the theoretical context by which the ethic of justice is situated. In doing so, we articulate varying conceptions of justice,

Ethical Leadership and the Community College: Paradigms, Decision-Making, and Praxis, pages 51–66.

the primary forms of which justice is manifested, and discuss the perceptions of justice that undergird the ethic of justice paradigm.

VARYING CONCEPTIONS OF JUSTICE

The concept of justice has long served as *the* core focus of ethical standards among scholars and philosophers (George, 2010). However, there have been many descriptions of justice. For example, writing in the *Republic* around 360–380 B.C., Plato[1] illustrated the numerous definitions of justice in a dialogue between Socrates, Cephalus, Polemarchus, and Thrasymachus. The dialogue occurs at the home of Cephalus (an aging businessman). In summary, Cephalus asserted that good men avoid purposely or unintentionally misleading others, and they should not die having owed debts to other men. Socrates characterized Cephalus' statement as "to speak the truth and to pay your debts," and Cephalus agrees with this characterization. Socrates questions this definition, stating that, if a friend is infuriated, then it would be unjust to return weapons (or arms) to them to speak truthfully to them.

After Cephalus leaves the conversation, Socrates asks Polemarchus (Cephalus' son) his perception of justice. Polemarchus defended his father by citing Simonides (a revered poet) who argued that justice entailed the repayment of debts. Socrates questions this perception, asking whether one should return debts to enemies. Polemarchus extends that enemies should also receive what is owed to them; however, he noted that an enemy is owed evil. Polemarchus proffers his definition of justice, stating that "justice is the art that gives good to friends and evil to enemies." The dialogue continues with the entrance of Thrasymachus who presents another very contrary, definition of justice; "injustice, when on a sufficient scale, has more strength and freedom and mastery than justice; and, as I said at first, *justice is the interest of the stronger.*"[2] Thrasymachus' definition characterizes those who are unjust as winners while those who are just as weak, friendless, losers. To illustrate his point, he provided examples where (on private contracts, taxes, and political office) the unjust have greater advantage, success, and power. Thus, for Thrasymachus, injustice is redefined as justice.

Of course, beyond these arguments, there are many other notions of justice that describe justice as: synonymous with love (Fletcher, 1966), a radical transformation of social structures, norms, and power that actualizes equity for all (McLaren, 1995; Sleeter, 1996); selfless enactment of one's social responsibilities (Cicero, 1913); restoring balance and maintaining peace in the social and metaphysical order (Ramose, 1999), acting in a manner that coexists with the freedom of others (Kant, 1996), and the benefit of the majority (Mills, 2003). As made clear, definitions of justice can vary greatly. In addition to multiple definitions of justice,

---

[1] Quotes derived from B. Jowett's (n.d.) translation of the *Republic*.
[2] Italics added for emphasis.

there are also multiple forms of justice that must be considered. As such, the next section overviews different forms of justice.

FIVE FORMS OF JUSTICE

Chryssides and Kaler (1996) articulated five primary forms of justice: procedural, substantive, retributive, remedial, and distributive. *Procedural justice* entails the equitable application of law in a manner that is neutral, objective, and fair. Typically, this form of justice is discussed in context of due process, the carrying out of law in a procedural context. Due process provides a formalized process where both sides of a dispute or issue can present their best cases (e.g., arguments, witnesses, evidence, etc.). In the American viewpoint of procedural justice, individuals are considered innocent until proven guilty through formal due process proceedings. Of course, in a collegiate context, procedures for due process can vary. For example, in academic misconduct procedures, students are often viewed as guilty until proven innocent. No matter the derivation, justice in this context refers to ensuring that due process procedures are adhered to in a manner which is fair for all parties involved.

Substantive justice refers to the fairness of rules, codes, policies, and standards. Thus, while procedural justice refers to the application of law, substantive justice refers to the justness of those laws by which fairness is judged. As such, substantive justice refers to the actions and critical questioning of the law to ensure that parity is upheld through the law. In a college context, rules and policies are often created through the process of shared governance (or other form of representative democracy). This process ensures that laws (broadly defined) are created mutually by faculty, students, staff, and administrators. Of course, in reality, the balance of power and representation in decision-making bodies does not always accurately

TABLE 5.1. Five forms of justice, goals and foci

	Procedural	Substantive	Retributive	Remedial	Distributive
Goal	Equitable application of law	To maintain fair laws	Maintaining order in society	Restoring balance to society	Fair benefits and disadvantages
Focus	Fairness for all parties involved	Creating and upholding fair rules	Punishment for wrong-doing	Remedying or repairing injustices	Equitable distribution of law
Example	Following hiring practices as described by human resource policies	Creating policies through shared governance reflective of varied interests and needs of stakeholders	Dismissing a student for violating academic honesty policies	Reinstating a faculty who did not receive tenure due to racism	Appropriating equal resources to academic departments with equal needs

reflect the people who will live under the constraints of those laws. For example, student voices are often absent or powerless in shared-governance processes. As such, policies are typically developed by campus affiliates (e.g., faculty, staff, and administration) that serve to benefit those at the decision-making table. Regardless of who is involved in decision-making, there remains a moral obligation to ensure that policies created are fair for all parties affected by them.

Retributive justice focuses on punitive actions for those who violate existing laws and codes. In order to maintain order in an organization, one must adhere to laws and codes. When these existing laws or codes are violated, punishments for violations are to be implemented in accordance with existing standards. Often, there are varying degrees of punishments that can be exacted for a given violation. Punishments should be applied with a focus on fairness and consistency. In some instances, the laws or codes in place will require that a punishment, based on extenuating circumstances or well-intentioned, but flawed policies (e.g., zero tolerance), mandate a higher punishment than seems sensible. Such instances, require the adherence to existing laws, but illustrate how substantive considerations can result in revisions to existing laws and policies to create parity for future cases. In all, retributive justice requires "striking the appropriate balance between the extremes of severity and leniency" (McFarlane, 2001, p. 144).

Remedial justice (also referred to as restorative justice) is concerned with remedying or repairing injustices that have occurred. Typically, remedial justice takes the form of compensation (e.g., admission of guilt, request for forgiveness, community service, money, etc.) that counterbalances injustices. In order to ensure fairness in the determination of remedial recourse, the perpetrator(s) of the injustice also has rights that must be honored. Often, the amount or degree of compensation will differ based on the intentionality of the injustice, with intentional injustices resulting in greater compensation than accidental or unintentional injuries. Remedial compensation can also be dependent upon the actor who created the injustice. Generally, when a state or institution is the perpetrator of injustice, the scrutiny and responsibility to correct the injustice is greater than when the injustice occurs at the individual level (that is, unless the individual is acting on behalf of the state). The goal in either case is the restoration of the recipient(s) of the injustice (e.g., individuals, departments, etc.) in proportionality to the relationship that existed prior to the injury.

Distributive Justice refers to the equitable distribution of law, resources, and power among individuals and groups in society. Scholars of this form of justice are concerned with how decisions are made that serve to distribute benefits and disadvantages fairly. McFarlane (2001) noted that, in an academic context, this entails ensuring that students have fair access to faculty, staff, administrators and campus resources. He suggests that ensuring parity may require a restriction of relationship affiliations with individuals, with whom an individual likes and does not like, in order to achieve a delicate balance of equal access. There is a direct connection between distributive and procedural justice, as efforts to ensure parity in the distribution of resources have identified procedural (e.g., due process) concerns that foster equitable outcomes. While all the aforementioned conceptions of justice are central to providing a context for this chapter's presentation of an ethic of justice, distributive justice (along with procedural justice) has been the primary foci of justice scholars (Wood & Hilton, 2012). The next section provides further context for distributive justice, based on the work of John Rawls.

THE RAWLSIAN ARTICULATION OF JUSTICE

John Rawls is widely considered the father of contemporary justice theory (Robbins & Trabichet, 2009; Sabbagh, 2001; St. John, 2009), and subsequently, the ethic of justice (Maxcy, 2002; Oliver & Hioco, 2012; Simola, 2003; Wood & Hilton, 2012). Rawls was an ardent advocate of a social contract; this philosophy served as an underpinning for his work. In brief, the notion of a social contract (as described by Thomas Hobbes, John Locke and Jean-Jacques Rousseau(AU: Pls. cite)) suggests that individuals relinquish some personal rights to the society (or rulers) in exchange for other rights and protections. This contract is assumed to be based on agreement by free persons who jointly determine which rights are exchanged for which protections, and what will constitute just and unjust actions. Social contractarians hold high respect for individual rights.

Given this philosophical orientation, Rawls was critical of ethical paradigms that placed the benefits (or greater good) of society over the rights of the individual. In doing so, he argued that such theories (particularly utilitarianism) can result in certain individuals being treated poorly (e.g., slavery, de jure segregation, meaning separation is enforced by law, etc.) as a means to benefit the interest of the masses over that of the individual (Robbins & Trabichet, 2009). He criticizes this perspective, noting that "a loss of freedom for some is not made right by a greater sum of satisfactions enjoyed by many" (Rawls, 2003, p. 155). Maxcy (2002) has noted that Rawls advocated the notion of a *veil of ignorance*, in which rules are made from a standpoint where presuppositions, socio-economic advantages, and talents are discarded. From this standpoint, one then asks: What would be the most just resolution once the veil is lifted? Based on this notion, Rawl's work emphasizes rational judgment, even when competing interests are involved (Oliver & Hioco, 2012). Rawls extended two principles of justice that have served as the framework for contemporary scholarship and critique of an ethic of justice. He stated that:

> first, each person engaged in an institution or affected by it has an equal right to the most extensive liberty compatible with a like liberty for all; and second, inequalities as defined by the institutional structure or fostered by it are arbitrary unless it is reasonable to expect that they will work out to everyone's advantage and provided that the positions and offices to which they attach or from which they may be gained are open to all. (p. 157)

TABLE 5.2. Two Principles of Justice

	Principle 1	Principle 2
Descriptor	Compatible Liberty	Difference Principle
Focus	Equal treatment	Equality of opportunity
Goal	Like liberty for all	Alleviating burdens for the disadvantaged
Values	Personal liberty Political parity Freedom of conscience Liberty of creed	Accountability Equity
Examples	Standardized assessment testing Academic credit review procedures Hiring and firing protocols	Educational opportunity programs Test-taking modifications for students with disabilities Preference given to diverse applicants

Rawls asserted that the first principle held primary priority among his principles. Simply stated, the first principle implies that justice requires an equal liberty for all individuals. Rawls suggested that four basic guidelines were needed to ensure the utility of the first principle; that there is personal liberty, political parity, freedom of conscience, and liberty of creed. Given this, Rawls conception of justice has been described as egalitarian (Lamont & Favor, 2013; Nagel, 1973). *Egalitarianism* holds that resources and goods be equally distributed among all members of society. Given the lexical ordering of his principles, equal distribution (irrespective of context) is the priority in promoting a just society. This notion invokes images of the portrayal of the goddess Lady Justice with a blindfold, illustrating the objectivity and fairness commonly associated with a justice-oriented approach.

Rawls second principle allows for *some* departure from the first principle. The second principle, referred to as the *difference principle* suggests that inequalities in society (i.e., providing more resources for one group over another) are only just if they are inculcated in a larger social plan to advance the interests of society's most needy individuals. The difference principle exists only "to alleviate as far as possible the arbitrary handicaps resulting from our initial starting places in society" (pp. 159–160). Rawls was clear that the difference principle was only permitted if it actually resulted in alleviating burdens for the disadvantaged to the point of improving their probability (or expectations) of success. He suggested that, as a mechanism to evaluate the utility of an intervention, that a reference point be selected that can serve as a barometer of success. He noted that this reference point should be "consistent with the demands of equal liberty and *equality of opportunity*" (p. 158).[3] Two primary points can be made here, first, Rawlsian justice places an emphasis on accountability as the difference principle requires a demonstration that social 'handicaps' are alleviated. Those in power are accountable to illustrate, through

---

[3] Italics added for emphasis.

Rawls improved expectations criteria that disadvantages (particularly those that are socio-economic) are remedied through actions which employ inequality to promote equity. Note here too, that equality of opportunity is the ideal. *Equality of opportunity* here refers to resolving limitations in competitive prospects produced by one's natural-born socio-economic status. Hence, (we assert that) equality of opportunity has a very restrictive definition. Influenced by Rawls writings, the ethic of justice is a primary ethical decision-making lens. Guided by the prior context, the next section defines and describes the ethic of justice.

ETHIC OF JUSTICE DEFINED

The *Ethic of Justice* is an ethical paradigm grounded in the notion that the 'right' decision in a given circumstance will be rooted in the "rule of law and the more abstract concepts of fairness, equity, and justice" (Shapiro & Stefkovich, 2005, p. 13). A justice-oriented leader conceptualizes problems, interprets phenomena, and approaches ethical dilemmas from this perspective. There are two core aspects of this definition, 'the rule of law,' and the 'concepts of fairness, equity, and justice.' With respect to the prior, the *rule of law* refers to established guidelines, specifically, laws and codes, policies, procedures, and standards. From this perspective, justice is associated with these guidelines which are used as the primary drivers of decision-making (Vogel, 2012). As such, Beckner (2004) refers to an ethic of justice as a 'rule-based' decision-making perspective. Justice-oriented leaders rely upon, affirm, and believe in the rule of law, which they propagate as *the* platform to actualize fair treatment through an even application of universal standards (Robbins & Trabichet, 2009).

The second component of this definition is that the concepts of equity, fairness, and justice are primarily interpreted through the lenses of uniformity and individual rights (Skoe & von der Lippe, 2002). With respect to uniformity (hereafter referred to as fairness), all individuals (e.g., administrators, faculty, staff, students) are treated the same within their respective groups, without regard for racial/ethnic, gender, or socio-economic status. Some have referred to this perspective as "the application of universal principles to moral decisions" (Enomoto, 1997, p. 353), "a practice of uniformity," (Robbins & Trabichet, 2009), and "an identical share" (Olsen, 1997, p. 627). As such, justice entails equal treatment of individuals. Hence, justice is distributed with exact similitude. This is similar to McFarlane's (2001) argument that justice entails ensuring that students have fair access to faculty, staff, administrators and campus resources. McFarlane notes that in achieving this idea, leaders should follow Levanthal's (1980) *bias suppression rule*, where campus leaders are cautious to ensure that favoritism is avoided in policy or practice, and that preferences are suppressed.

Contrary to this perspective, many community colleges provide early course registration opportunities for students who participated in summer-bridge (or other transitional) programming. This benefit is designed to incentivize program participation for students who are predominantly first-generation and low-income.

TABLE 5.3. Ethic of Justice Components, Core Principles and Leadership Benefits

Primary leadership style	Bureaucratic	
Focus of ethical standard	Non-Consequentialist (means)	
Frame of Reference	The rule of law	
Objective	Order, efficiency, and stability	
Key Values/Virtues	Fairness, parity, and justice	
Theoretical Underpinning(s)	Rawl's writings on Justice	
Primary Question	What do the rules and policies say?	
Core Principles	1.	The rule of law
	2.	Uniform Fairness
	3.	Accountability
	4.	Individual Rights
	5.	Rational Decision-Making
	6.	Moral Objectivity
	7.	Clarity through Law
Leadership Benefits*	1.	Clarity of Law
	2.	Certainty in Law
	3.	Efficiency of Practice
	4.	Consistency of Application
	5.	Maintenance of the Status Quo
	6.	Reduced Organizational Liability
	7.	Organizational Stability

Note: (*) derived from our reflections and the works of: Enomoto (1997), Shapiro and Gross (2009), Simola (2003).

However, from a perspective of justice, providing early registration for some students and not others would not be perceived as equitable as it prioritizes certain students over others. Thus, a justice-oriented leader would be apprehensive (at least initially) in supporting such programming. A justice-oriented leader is guided by the rule of law, so programming that has been approved through official channels and processes would be implemented. Moreover, while this example illustrates that justice leaders are focused on uniformity; at the same time, they are also not interested in creating rules that would serve to marginalize or disadvantage one group over another (Oliver & Hioco, 2012). As a consequence, there is a focus on creating laws that neither serve to advantage nor disadvantage individuals in society.

From a Rawlsian perspective, the leader prioritizes 'equal liberty' for all; thus, the 'difference principle' (which allows for providing additional support for the underserved) should only be enacted if the program would serve to benefit all by alleviating the barriers for the most needy students. As such, in decision-making discussions around the allocation of extra programs or resources for a needy population, leaders would give preference to interventions that could *demonstrate* the potential/

ability to: alleviate burdens associated with one's initial status in life; and enhance one's expectations of success in relationship to the reference population. As such, an ethic of justice is associated with accountability. This notion is perceivable in two primary ways. Firstly, when the 'difference principle' is employed, they are accountable to ensure that programs created for underserved and marginalized communities must, in fact, actually work to remedy initial life differences. Secondly, they are accountable to upholding parity in the rule of law (Rawls first principle), as it pertain to the various forms of justice (e.g., procedural, substantive, retributive, remedial, and distributive). In doing so, they are cognizant of their accountability to governing boards, superiors (e.g., Presidents, Vice Presidents, Deans, Directors, faculty), and to the general public who have entrusted them with the duties of their office. However, the tendency of justice leaders is to revert to mainstream practices, particularly as it relates to equity programs that do not possess adequate data to demonstrate the utility of the intervention.

Moreover, from a justice perspective, an important byproduct of uniformity as a proxy for fairness is the integrity of individual rights (Simola, 2003). Because absolute standards of judgment validate appropriate courses of action, individual rights are not subject to the rights of the community or greater good. Rather, parity between the individual and the community is sought (referred to as a 'dualistic tension,' Begley & Stefkovich, 2007). For example, "ethical issues such as due process and privacy rights are often balanced against the need for civility and the good of the majority" (Shapiro & Stefkovich, 2005, p. 13). Starratt (1991) discussed the nuances and complexities of maintaining this balance; he stated that educational leaders must address concerns regarding individual rights such as academic grievances, discipline policies, and "faculty time commitments," while also addressing community-related concerns such as curricula, course materials, extracurricular programming, and standardized mechanisms of assessment (p. 194).

An ethic of justice emphasizes rational decision-making that is morally objective. In practice, this means that justice is "determined by weighing competing rights within a rubric of absolute moral injunctions" (Doscher & Normore, 2005, p. 12). Decisions are rational in that they are based on reasoned interpretation of facts. As such, this approach de-emphasizes the role of emotion in addressing dilemmas (Enomoto, 1997). A justice framework is morally objective in that established standards (based on the rule of law) are pre-determined (Beckner, 2004), and are employed as absolute and unbiased standards of action (Simola, 2003). These standards are unbiased as they are in existence before ethical quandaries are encountered, thereby mitigating the influence of personal and professional interest as well as cultural inclinations (Beckner, 2004). Given this, the ethic of justice has been referred to as a non-consequentialist framework, meaning that leaders do not consider the outcomes or byproducts of the actions they take (Northouse, 2007; Strike, Haller, & Soltis, 2005).

The outcome of a given decision (e.g., dismissing a student from college, denying a faculty member tenure, etc.) is not of concern as the 'right' course of action is based on rules, codes, regulations and other standards of judgment. Leaders still hope for positive outcomes; however, mechanisms by which decisions are made are of greater importance (Nevarez, Wood, & Penrose, 2013), as leaders have a moral responsibility to adhere to the rule of law (Maxcy, 2002). While justice-oriented leaders maintain the rule of law regardless of outcome, they recognize that laws, codes, policies, and standards can (at times) result in unjust outcomes. While imperfect, they believe that law and policy continually improves over time (Delgado, 1995). When this occurs, the leader continues to enforce the rule of law; however, they may also work to change the law through formal processes (e.g., mandate, shared-governance, collective bargaining, etc.). In doing so, the law is maintained throughout this process until it has been officially modified or eliminated.

Postsecondary institutions are often bureaucratic in nature. As such, there are numerous rules, codes, and policies that can serve to guide leaders' decision-making. Ethic of justice leaders benefit from this structure as they rely upon clarity through the law. However, there are two common challenges that ethic of justice leaders face in adhering to the rule of law. Firstly, in many circumstances, there will be no evident policy in place which can guide decision-making. As a result, the leader is left without a specific guide for action. Secondly, due to the proliferation of rules and codes within complex organizational structures, ethic of justice leaders may also face circumstances where the policies that are in place will be unclear or conflict with other policies. In these cases, justice leaders attempt to resolve the dilemma based on prior actions and/or comparable policies with similar concerns that seem equivalent. Again, the focus here is on fairness and equal application of the law. After the dilemma has been addressed, ethic of justice leaders work through formal democratic processes to create laws and policies that will provide clear guidance to addressing similar concerns in the future. To avoid this reactive position, ethic of justice leaders have a clear understanding of the rule of law. Based on this understanding, they work to create and refine rules, policies, and procedures in advance as to limit the occurrence of policy misalignment and loop-holes.

Bearing the aforementioned in mind, an ethic of justice is situated within the social domain, governing actions, decisions, and behaviors relevant to the public arena (Enomoto, 1997). Given that community colleges encompass a social and physical space in this domain, the ethic of justice framework can serve as a foundational ethical guide. Using this lens, the following questions serve as typical decision-making considerations for leaders who employ an ethic of justice framework:

- What laws, codes, policies, procedures and standards are in place?
- What decision would enforce and honor these permutations of the rule of law?
- Which decision will ensure that every individual is treated the same?
- Which decision will respect individual rights while maximizing the general welfare?
- What will result in the outcome that is most fair or equal?

The next section describes the benefits associated for leaders who ascribe to an ethic of justice paradigm.

BENEFITS OF AN ETHIC OF JUSTICE

The ethic of justice has been the object of much critique, berated by critical and feminist scholars as a 'detached,' oppressive, and patriarchal decision-making framework (see chapter on Ethic of Care, Doscher & Normore, 2005). However, from a pragmatic standpoint, this lens has many strengths, including: the right course of action among many other possible actions is well-defined by pre-established standards (clarity); there is added confidence that the decision being made is the correct decision (certainty); dilemmas can be resolved quickly (efficiency), and future problems will be addressed in a like manner (consistency) (Enomoto, 1997; Nevarez & Wood, 2010; Simola, 2003). Moreover, given the increasingly litigious nature of society and the enhanced scrutiny of public institutions, universal treatment of individuals can reduce institutional exposure to lawsuits. Another, more controversial benefit of a justice orientation is asserted by Enotomo (1997). She noted that reliance on the ethic of justice benefits leaders by maintaining the 'status quo.' The political pitfalls of leadership, especially in the current climates of accountability, decreasing revenues, and competition can serve to provide stability to organizational climates that are unstable. Thus, leaders employing a justice framework can curb *some* of the challenges of ethical leadership in turbulent times (see Shapiro & Gross, 2008). This may be of particular importance for organizational affiliates (e.g., faculty, staff, and students) who have recently experienced institutional crises, reorganization, or leadership turnover. Given the benefits of an ethic of justice, we suggest some basic steps individuals can take to become better justice-oriented leaders.

DEVELOPING A JUSTICE ORIENTATION

There are several strategies that leaders can employ to develop their analysis of ethical dilemmas in line with the justice tradition. Firstly, leaders can become familiar with the extant laws, policies, procedures, and standards that govern their institutions. In long form, this includes a keen understanding of:

a. federal, state, and local laws and codes created by and through the legislative process, executive authority, judicial rulings, and other democratically empowered entities (e.g., county boards, city council, etc.);

b. educational policies established by state governing entities, boards of trustees, campus administration, as well as regulations manifested through the shared governance and collective bargaining processes;

c. documented procedures for human resource, administrative, fiscal, and academic matters; and

d. standards established by national, regional, and disciplinary accreditation agencies, regardless of voluntary or compensatory affiliation.

Secondly, given the rapidly changing nature of laws, justice leaders should establish practices that enable them to be up to date on rule updates and proposed changes. Likely, this will include setting aside a regular time for periodic review of new and proposed legal modifications which includes having a mechanized process for receiving information blasts from policy groups, the *Chronicle of Higher Education, Community College Times*, and *Inside Higher Education*. Leaders can work closely with human resources and legal counsel to interpret the impact of new and proposed policy changes, with a specific focus on the potential impact on day-to-day practices.

Thirdly, based on an enhanced understanding of the rule of law, identify loopholes in the law, as well as policies that are either lacking clarity or having points of conflict. Then, propose remedies to these issues through your college's formal democratic process. In addition, consider creating or revising a handbook (in tandem with colleagues) that governs practice in your respective department (e.g., counseling, academic programs, etc.). Then, work to have this handbook or your revisions to an existing handbook formally recognized.

Fourthly, practice bias suppression by making rational decisions that are informed by an objective analysis of fact and restrict emotional responses during decision-making processes. Doing so for some will require extensive practice (especially those who lead with their hearts); however, this is a key skillset needed for success in administration. Moreover, in light of leaders' focus on accountability, established practices that monitor the effectiveness of policies through evaluation must be implemented, particularly for equity-based programs and services.

In addition to these suggested steps, leaders should become attuned to their own leadership dispositions and practice problem solving from an ethic of justice lens. This chapter provides three resources to support the reader's development of a justice-orientation. In the following section, discussion questions are provided that can enable readers to gauge their understanding of the information presented in this chapter. Readers should begin to consider their own beliefs in relation to this chapter's content. At the end of this chapter, the *Ethic of Justice Leadership Inventory* (Nevarez & Wood, 2013) is presented. Use this inventory to learn more about your own leadership preferences. This inventory will provide you information needed to begin the process of critical introspection of your own actions, behaviors, and mores. Then, use the case study presented at the end of this chapter to practice addressing problems from an ethic of justice lens.

DISCUSSION QUESTIONS

1. This chapter presented many different definitions of justice. How do you personally define justice? What principles or characteristics do you employ in your own pursuit of justice?

2. As noted, there are five primary forms of justice: procedural, substantive, retributive, remedial, and distributive. What are some challenges you or

your organization face in maintaining the rule of law and fairness in each of these respective areas?

3. What are your thoughts about the bias suppression rule? What are the strengths and weaknesses of this approach? How do you perceive leaders who engage in bias suppression?

4. This chapter provided some benefits to an ethic of justice leadership approach. Do you believe there are additional benefits to this paradigm? If so, what are they? Moreover, what are the weaknesses (if any) of an ethic of justice paradigm?

5. Based on your reading of this chapter, what are some questions that you can ask yourself when approaching a dilemma from an ethic of justice lens?

DEFINITIONS

Bias Suppression Rule: suppression of one's preferences in the carrying out of one's duties in order to maintain uniform fairness.

Difference Principle: suggests that inequities in society are only justifiable if they are inculcated in a larger social plan to advance the interests of society's most needy.

Distributive Justice: refers to the equitable distribution of law, resources, and power among individuals and groups in society.

Egalitarianism: holds that resources and goods be equally distributed among all members of society, irrespective of context.

Equality of Opportunity: refers to resolving limitations in competitive prospects produced by one's natural born socio-economic status.

Procedural Justice: entails the equitable application of law in a manner that is neutral, objective, and fair.

Remedial Justice: is concerned with remedying or repairing injustices that have occurred.

Retributive Justice: focuses on punitive actions for those who violate existing laws and codes.

Rule of Law: refers to established guidelines, specifically, laws and codes, policies, procedures, and standards.

Substantive Justice: refers to the fairness of rules, codes, policies, and standards.

Veil of Ignorance: where rules are made from a standpoint where presuppositions, socio-economic advantages, and talents are discarded.

NEVAREZ & WOOD: ETHIC OF JUSTICE LEADERSHIP INVENTORY (NW-EJLI)

This leadership inventory is designed to aid leaders in assessing their use of ethical leadership theory. Ethical leaders strive to make the 'right' decisions; however, perspectives on the method(s) of reaching the 'right' decision can differ. While there are a number of differing ethical paradigms, this inventory focuses on the ethic of justice. Current leaders should reflect on actions that they typically take and perceptions that they hold. Aspiring leaders should consider the actions that they would take if they held a formal leadership position within an organization. Read the following statements and mark the appropriate response. If you find statements difficult to answer, trust your instinct and judgment in selecting the most appropriate response. Remember that there are no right or wrong answers:

	Strongly Disagree (1 pt)	Disagree (2 pts)	Somewhat Disagree (3 pts)	Somewhat Agree (4 pts)	Agree (5 pts)	Strongly Agree (6 pts)
1. Having strong rules, policies, and procedures will always lead to better organizational outcomes.						
2. Leaders should always adhere to the rules and regulations in place.						
3. Following a policy is more important than the outcome of the policy.						
4. In all cases, the "right" thing to do is to follow the rules, polices, and protocols in place.						
5. I establish codes and policies for my staff and expect them to be followed at all times.						
6. Organizational success is facilitated through a strong chain of command.						
7. Leaders' should enact new policies when there are areas without policy guidance.						
8. Handbooks should clearly delineate each individual's areas of responsibility.						
9. Employees should never circumvent the organizational structure.						

	Strongly Disagree (1 pt)	Disagree (2 pts)	Somewhat Disagree (3 pts)	Somewhat Agree (4 pts)	Agree (5 pts)	Strongly Agree (6 pts)
10. It is the leader's responsibility to direct and the followers responsibility to carry out orders.						

Note: This inventory is printed with permission from the Nevarez-Wood Community College Leadership Institute. All rights reserved.

Scoring

To score your responses, do the following: add up the total sum of your responses for all of the questions in the inventory. This is your total ethic of justice leadership score. Higher scores indicated greater levels of justice orientation. In contrast, lower scores indicate lower levels of justice orientation. The maximum score possible is 60.

_____ *Total Justice Leadership Score*

SCORE MEANING

While the maximum score is 60, many leaders may desire to understand their usage of this framework in comparison to other leaders. To facilitate this interest, scores from prior inventory participants were divided into percentile ranges. These percentile ranges allow leaders to understand their score in relation to other leaders. The percentile ranges are as follows: Low justice orientation (33rd percentile or lower); Medium justice orientation (34th to 66th percentile), and High justice orientation (67th to 99th percentile).

- Low justice orientation: 10 to 30 points
- Medium justice orientation: 31 to 40 points
- High justice orientation: 41 to 60 points

Total score should be contextualized in light of scores gathered from additional ethical inventories in this volume. In doing so, leaders are provided with a more accurate depiction of their ethical standing across the four primary paradigms. Ideally, equivalent orientations scores (medium, high) across all paradigms depict a well-balanced orientation. Consistency of orientation levels across the four paradigms reflects leaders' ability to be multi-oriented and multi-skilled in using ethical paradigms to effectively engage in leadership and organizational decision-making.

RELIABILITY

Two internal consistency estimates were employed to examine the reliability of the justice leadership inventory: split-half coefficient and coefficient alpha. For the split-half reliability, the scale was divided into equal halves for item equivalency. We took into account the order of the measures; thus, the sequence of items was rotated. One half included items 1, 3, 5, 7, and 9, while the second half included items 2, 4, 6, 8, and 10. The split-half coefficient was .81 while the coefficient alpha was .84. Both procedures illustrated satisfactory reliability.

SUGGESTED CITATION

Nevarez, C., & Wood, J. L. (2013). *Nevarez & Wood—Ethic of Justice leadership inventory (NW- EJLI)*. Sacramento, CA: Nevarez-Wood Community College Leadership Institute.

NOTE

In the validation sample for this inventory, ethic of justice scores were negatively correlated with leaders self-assessment of their leadership ability, critical thinking, initiative, social ability, and level of influence. Ethic of justice total scores had a negative correlation with ethic of critique scores ($r = -0.48$). A shorter version of the ethic of justice inventory is published as a scale in Nevarez, Wood, and Penrose (2013) *Leadership Theory and the Community College*. Stylus Publication.

CHAPTER 6

THE ETHIC OF CRITIQUE

This chapter highlights the development of Critical Theory as articulated by the Frankfurt School. The authors discuss how critical theory is defined and overview thematic trends emanating from the writings of critical theorists. Using this foundation, the ethic of critique is extended as an ethical paradigm derived from critical theory. Leaders employing this paradigm are critical of societal inequities and are committed to uncovering, challenging, and overcoming inequities through social justice. The primary elements of this ethical lens are discussed in relationship to community college leadership.

When reading this chapter, consider the following questions:

- What is critical theory?
- What are some primary schools of thought emanating from critical theory?
- What are the strengths and limitations of an ethic of critique?
- In what way (if any) can this framework enhance your leadership and inform institutional change?

CRITICAL THEORY: THE FRANKFURT SCHOOL

In the 1920s and 1930s, western European scholars of the Marxist tradition formed the Institute for Social Research (Therborn, 1996). The Institute was funded by

---

Ethical Leadership and the Community College: Paradigms, Decision-Making, and Praxis, pages 67–84.

Hermann Weil a rich grain merchant whose son, Felix Weil, was an ardent advocate for the founding of the institute (Carr, 2000). In the summer of 1922, Felix hosted a summit called the First Marxist Work Week, which brought together scholars and socialist leaders for a week-long discourse on pure Marxism. Felix was so invigorated by the summit that he set out to establish a permanent institute for critical scholarship and discourse (Jay, 1973). The Institute was affiliated with the University of Frankfurt in Frankfurt am Main, Germany; however, it was financially independent from the University. Carl Grünberg, a legal and political scholar served as the first director of the institute (Carr, 2000). The scholars were affiliated with this Institute and their resultant body of work is collectively referred to as the Frankfurt School (Thernborn, 1996). This school of thought is most commonly associated with the works of Theodor Adorno, Herbert Marcuse, Friedrich Pollock, Erich Fromm, and influenced the works of Jürgen Habermas and Antonio Gramsci. Chief among them was Max Horkheimer, who served as the Institute director beginning in the 1930s. A key element of Horkheimer's perspective was that critical inquiry should exhaustively investigate social inequities through interdisciplinary lenses which give light to the numerous manifestations and effects of such inequities.

As a whole, the aforementioned critical theorists observed the carnage of World War I (Therborn, 1996). They also witnessed the Soviet brand of socialism. They were critical of this polity, which they criticized for sacrificing aims for survivalism. In particular, they were concerned with the totalitarian restriction of literary freedom that they perceived as manifesting oppression rather than reducing it. They were also critical contemporary Marxists scholars who were becoming increasingly dogmatic, zealous ideologues. They saw this as having the potential to perpetuate absolutism, which they perceived as inhibiting social progress. These theorists also saw the spread and ubiquitous might of capitalism. In particular, they observed the rapid growth of capitalistic mega-monopolies in Western Europe. Moreover, they encountered expansive ethnic oppression via fascism with the rise of Adolph Hitler and the Nazi regime in Germany. Given that the Institute was predominated by Jewish academicians, the latter, resulted in the exile of the Frankfurt scholars to Geneva and New York, and the seizure of their 60,000 volume library (Jay, 1973). This context is provided to express the historical and philosophical context in which critical theory emerged.

As noted, Marxism serves as the theoretical underpinning and provides the "methods and tools" by which criticalists interpret the world (Carr, 2000, p. 210). According to Marx and Engel's (1848/1999), civilization is best understood through an analysis of production based upon the powers (materials and resources) and social powers (the group which controls the materials and resources) of production. Marxists situate the focus of their analyses on the economy. They assert that economic systems (e.g., capitalism, feudalism, etc.) structure the human social condition. Thus, society is best understood through economicism. For Marxists, society is bifurcated into two components, base and superstructure. Simplistically conceptualized, *base* refers to economic systems and the interrelations among divergent economic systems. *Superstructure* is the social structure that exists on this base, including government, social institutions, laws and codes, social relations, culture, and the arts. Base serves to influence the superstructure, further reifying the base (though criticalists see this relationship as bidirectional). Marxists perceived that society was divided into two primary class structures: the bourgeoisie (wealthy oppressors and owners of capital); and the proletariat (the dominated poor and workers of production). The focus on economicism, power relations, social stratification, and superstructure are all evident in the writings of criticalists.

The early criticists were also influenced by Hegelian thought. Specifically, the notion of 'moment' (also referred to as dialectic) influenced their thinking. Dialectic logic is derived from three integrated processes involving thesis, anti-thesis, and synthesis— or as referred to by Marx (1978) as affirmation, negation, and negation of the negation. Simplistically, an argument (thesis) is subjected to counter-arguments (anti-thesis) until a revised and improved argument is made (synthesis). In Marxism, this notion was employed in the study of ideas, theories, values, traditions, and political movements (among other domains), where the greater economic context served as the framework for this dialectical process. These ideas greatly influenced early criticists, who have been referred to as western Marxists or Hegelian-Marxists (Bohman, 2005; Carr, 2000; Therborn, 1996).

DEFINING CRITICAL THEORY

Guided by the aforementioned, critical theory assumes that subjugation is inherent in society. The notion is adeptly captured by Peter McLaren (2003), who stated that "Critical theorists begin with the premise that men and women are essentially unfree, and inhabit a world rife with contradictions and asymmetries of power and privilege" (p. 69). This perspective is best understood considering critical theory emerged from a historical context of oppression. Its intellectual founders were keenly attuned to injustice, directly experiencing the effects of anti-Semitism and holding negative evaluations of the effect of capitalism on the proletariat. Despite this deleterious perspective on the human social condition, critical theory is action-oriented. For example, Horkheimer (1982) extended the most commonly recognized definition of critical theory. He stated that *critical theory* is a school of thought driven by the aim "to liberate human beings from the circumstances that enslave them" (Horkheimer, 1982, p. 244). As such, critical theory is emancipatory in nature. Defining the tenets of critical theory is, to a large degree, a difficult enterprise as its thinkers were/are ardently anti-dogmatic, rejecting absolutisms. However, across the body of work emanating from critical scholars, several thematic tendencies have emerged. These tendencies are explored in the next section.

THEMATIC ELEMENTS OF CRITICAL THOUGHT

Despite the aforementioned disclaimer, we present some thematic elements of critical theory. These elements are certainly not exhaustive, but represent an amalgamation of ideas from various critical thinkers (e.g., Bohman, 2005; Giroux,

1988; Horkheimer, 1993; Kellner, 2003; Kincheloe & McLaren, 2002; Therborn, 1996). The themes presented include: an assumption of oppression, social justice, and multiplicity of marginality.

An *assumption of oppression* refers to criticalists core belief that oppression and subjugation are inherent in the human social condition. This oppression occurs at the macro and micro levels, and is designed to affirm, sustain, and extend power inequities. In this light, all social institutions (e.g., schools, community colleges, universities, etc.) serve as sites for the reproduction of social stratification and relations (Giroux, 1988). *Critical enlightenment* refers to critical theorists' foci on illuminating power interests and relations in society. This term is derived from Kincheloe and McLaren's (2002) articulation of the elements of critical theory. They asserted that society is comprised of numerous power dynamics where those in power seek to maintain their power, often by perpetuating a status quo which reifies their power. Thus, the goal of criticists is to understand these dynamics, the individual(s) and group(s) that are advantaged or disadvantaged, and how this power is imbedded within the social order. The focus of such inquiry is often centered (though not exclusively) on class-, race-, and gender-based lenses. Criticalists seek to understand individual and group psychological processes that counter and advance social progress. However, critical theorists do not simply recognize that oppression occurs and study it; rather, criticists' aims are much loftier. Critical theory is social justice-oriented (Kellner, 2003; Therborn, 1996). *Social justice* refers to critical theorists' commitment to emancipating and empowering society's oppressed. This aim of critical theory is accomplished through enhanced moral agency while maintaining a sense of connection with others (Kellner, 2003; Kincheloe & McLaren, 2002; Therborn, 1996). Therefore, the role of educators is to transform educational institutions into locales for empowerment; rather than factories which fulfill the hierarchical needs of a stratified society.

In distancing themselves from establishing universal principles, critical theorists' affirm Marxist ideals while rejecting assumptions that economic systems are the sole framework for understanding and countering oppression (Kincheloe & McLaren, 2002). Like Marxism, critical theory places economic systems and the superstructure as essential elements of social analysis. Thus, fields such as education are examined in context of "the dominant social relations and system of political economy" (Kellner, 2003, p. 53). However, critical theorists remain concerned with other forms of oppression, marginalization, and alienation beyond that of class. They recognize the *multiplicity of marginality*, meaning that oppression is manifested, takes different forms, and evolves in different ways across different contexts. Regardless of whether critical theorists focus on issues of race, gender, class, disability (or other forms of marginality) they recognize that oppression itself is the underlying current by which social hierarchy is perpetuated. With this context in mind, we discuss an outgrowth of critical theory among ethicians, the ethic of critique.

THE ETHIC OF CRITIQUE DEFINED

Critical theory is the antecedent of the ethic of critique (Nevarez & Wood, 2010; Roubanis, Garner, & Purcell, 2008; Shapiro & Hassinger, 2007). Guided by the moral philosophy of this lens, the *ethic of critique* is defined as a decision-making paradigm which is critical of societal inequities, and is committed to uncovering, challenging, and overcoming inequities through social justice. The most influential depiction of the ethic of critique (among educational ethicists) was articulated by Robert Starratt (1991). Starratt noted that the ethic of critique serves as a framework for a comprehensive critique of "social relationships, social customs, laws, social institutions...power relations, or language itself" (Starratt, 1991, p. 189). Thus, no category within these domains (superstructure) is above criticism. As such, this ethic holds *critique* as a cardinal value for navigating the world of leadership. In the context of educational leadership, the critique is primarily centered at institutional bureaucracy, which is seen as propagating social reproduction, dehumanization, oppression, marginalization, and alienation. As a result, community college leaders employing this paradigm focus their efforts on critiquing and changing the bureaucratic elements of their institutions. This includes a critical view of bureaucratic elements such as; the difficult processes by which policies are made, the barrage of federal and state mandates, negotiations between faculty senates and faculty unions with the administration, and bureaucratic principles (e.g., uniform fairness, accountability).

In this light, the ethic of critique is a response to an ethic of justice. While justice leaders see the rule of law as the primary base for determining what is

TABLE 6.1.   Critical Strategies for Creating Equity Oriented Institutions

Primary leadership styles	Transformative
Focus of ethical standard	Consequentialist (ends)
Frame of Reference	Critique of law
Objective	Undoing injustice, inequity, and marginality
Key Values/Virtues	Social justice, emancipation, and equity
Theoretical Underpinning(s)	Critical Theory (and its manifestations)
Primary Question	How are we reifying injustice?
Core Principles	1. Assumption of Oppression 2. Social Responsibility 3. Identifying Inequities 4. Challenge Status Quo 5. Social Justice
Leadership Benefits	1. Emancipates the marginalized 2. Creating greater liberty for all within an organization 3. Better organizational decision-making 4. Greater dialogue and understanding

'right' or 'good,' an ethic of critique points to instances where laws, codes, and policies have created the opposite conditions. Specifically, criticalists are acutely aware of power differences that allowed for certain laws to be created, and how law is used as a tool to reaffirm and extend power (Roubanis et al., 2008). As such, while an ethic of justice perceives 'the rule of law' as fostering liberty, an ethic of critique sees it as a barrier to emancipation. Moreover, critical ethicians are concerned with the objective and rational decision-making principles of an ethic of justice. They perceive that objective rationality permits injustice by ignoring the consequences of decisions (Shapiro, 2006; Shapiro & Hassinger, 2007; Shapiro & Purpel, 2004). As such, while an ethic of justice is non-consequentialist, an ethic of critique is *consequentialist*, meaning that the *consequences* of outcomes or byproducts of a given decision are of primary concern (Northouse, 2007). In essence, the point of determining what is 'right' is based on the outcome, not the rule of law. From a Hegelian perspective, the ethic of critique is the antithesis of the thesis of bureaucracy. The goal, of this negation, is to produce a synthesis which creates better realities and outcomes for all.

ASSUMPTION OF OPPRESSION

An ethic of critique is associated with an assumption of oppression, believing that oppression and subjugation are inherent in the human social condition. Criticalists assert that social dynamics and interactions are typified by differential power as laws, customs, rationality legitimize, and reify oppression (Kellner, 2003; Kincheloe & McLaren, 2002; Therborn, 1996). For example, Starratt (1991) noted that "the critical ethician stresses...that no social arrangement is neutral. It is usually structured to benefit some segments of society at the expense of others" (p. 189). Nor, are social arrangements "culture-free" (Patton, 1998, p. 32). As such, when stratification is evident in social institutions, these institutions lack a reasonable framework by which to remedy those inequities (Furman, 2003). Starratt (1991) provides a strong articulation of this assumption. He noted that bureaucracy is the platform by which oppression is often manifested in educational contexts. To operate efficiently, bureaucracy inherently limits liberty, ingenuity, and individuality.

Moreover, Starratt (1991) suggests that "schools and school systems are structurally ineffective" (p. 188). In the community college context, this would suggest that community colleges, their districts, and coordinating bodies are structurally ineffective. One only needs to point to disparate outcomes among students, the academic-student affairs divide, articulation issues with four-year institutions, lack of intraorganizational linkages between certificate and associate programs, political infighting among and between faculty members and the administration, and increasing funding instability to illustrate these inefficiencies. Further, Starratt suggests that bureaucracy should be seen as an "enduring problem, not simply a contemporary phenomenon" (p. 189). In affirming this statement, he critiques bureaucracies, highlighting four attributes. He argues that bureaucracies are:

a.   adversarial—where power and interests conflict by station (e.g., faculty, staff, administrators, and students) and their characteristics (e.g., race, class, gender, etc.);

b.   hierarchical—in that different individuals and groups hold varying levels of power;

c.   impersonal—as bureaucratic objectivity and rationality overshadow experiences, disparaging realities, and inequitable outcomes; and

d.   technicist—where standardization of assessment, curriculum, and operations has devalued teaching and learning.

From a critical perspective, there is an interrelationship between social landscapes and opportunities and greater forces of production. As such, structural efficiencies are expected, in that they are not inefficiencies at all; as the greater forces (e.g., economic, racial, patriarchal, etc.) rely upon social hierarchy and advantage for sustainability. Thus, as sites of social reproduction, community colleges manifest stratification. Overwhelmingly, college professionals (e.g., faculty, staff, and administrators) are unconscious about their role in this reproduction. However, criticalists would point to the predominance of low-income and students of color in vocational certificate programs and their low transfer outcomes in comparison to their peers. Certainly, community colleges provide some students with opportunities for economic and social mobility, while tracking other students into low-wage, limited mobility, restricted autonomy work settings. This is often done under the banner of workforce development and training.

SOCIAL RESPONSIBILITY

Critical leaders believe in social responsibility. Starratt (1991) noted that this responsibility is "not simply to the individuals in the school or school system, not simply to the education profession, but to the society of whom, and for whom, he or she is an agent" (p. 191). As an agent of the institution, the critical leader understands that social responsibility is a moral imperative; that they, themselves, have the mantle of responsibility placed upon them to create greater parity for societies underserved. Starratt suggested that this calling is imbedded within their professional and legal duties to the people, institutions, and communities they serve. Given that educational institutions serve as centers for oppression and social reproduction, the responsibility of an ethic of critique leader is to "uncover this inequality, confront it, and begin to make bold social arrangements" that alter practice (Patton, 1998, p. 28). As such, an ethic of critique requires leaders to "uncover," "expose," and "redress such injustice" via social justice (p. 189).

As noted, an ethic of critique leader assumes that oppression is endemic to bureaucracy. Moreover, they understand that structural inequities are undergirded by, without fail, indefensible assumptions (Starratt, 1991). The goal then of a critical leader, is to identify structural inequities evident in the superstructure as well as the flawed assumptions by which they are fostered. When employing an ethic of critique, leaders are conscious of how social structures and practices serve to advantage certain individuals and groups over others (Furman, 2003). This critique extends to them personally, where they interrogate their own assumptions and biases as well as those commonly held within the institutions that they serve (George, 2010). This critique also encompasses the institutions they serve as well as social conditions in a wider society. For example, in a predominant English language-speaking state, those non-English speaking individuals are often more likely to be exploited and oppressed. According to Abrahamson (2006), an ethic of critique leaders would recognize that community colleges can serve as a platform to counter wider social challenges by preserving English as a Second Language courses, even in difficult financial landscapes.

IDENTIFYING INEQUITIES

Furman (2003; 2004) extends that an ethic of critique focuses on identifying barriers (e.g., policies, practices, language, values) which limit equitable experiences and outcomes for all individuals. Identifying barriers involves an understanding of privilege and oppression in the subtlest and most evident forms (Roubanis et al., 2008). In essence, critique leaders understand who are the 'have' and 'have nots' in a given social context. Therefore, the challenge for ethical leaders is to transform institutions and the people within to be more aware of social arrangements that foster inequities (Furman, 2004). A critical leader questions the origins of the rule of law, the interest of the people who create them, the presence or absence of voices at the decision-making table, and how rules serve to advantage and disadvantage certain groups over others. Aware of the multiplicity of marginality, the focus of their inquiry is on differential outcomes by race, class, gender, and other forms of marginality. This analysis requires critical leaders to "redefine and reframe categories such as privilege, power, culture, language, and in particular, social justice" (Shapiro & Hassinger, 2007, p. 453). However, critical leaders are also aware that oppression is complex, even within single institutions where one who is oppressed in one circumstance may serve as the oppressor in other circumstances. Identifying barriers to inclusion and equity are enhanced through data. Critical community college leaders can employ assessment, evaluation, and other modes of inquiry to document evidence of injustice. For instance, they can employ:

a.   needs evaluation to identify barriers to inclusion and success;
b.   process evaluation to evidence how monies, programs, and policies intended for greater equity are actually employed; and
c.   outcomes evaluation to illustrate differential academic (e.g., persistence, achievement, attainment, transfer) and affective outcomes differ by race, class, gender, disability and other forms of marginality.

In doing so, they can better articulate their critiques in technicist bureaucratic contexts.

CHALLENGE STATUS QUO

When inequities are uncovered, the role of an ethic of critique leader is to illuminate social conditions which manifest subjugation, alienation, isolation, and marginalization (Patton, 1998). A leader employing an ethic of critique challenges social norms. They avoid taken-for-granted assumptions and values, believing that social inequities are remedied through countering dominant ideologies (George, 2010; Roubanis et al., 2008). Challenging the status quo is pursued by illustrating to others the injustice that is occurring and why it is taking place. Specifically, this involves naming, showing evidence of, and creating recognition of structures and language which perpetuate these social inequities (Starratt, 1991). In challenging dominant ideologies, it is important to recognize that "theories, assumptions, and practices ...are enormously resistant to change" (Patton, 1998, p. 27). Thus, critical leaders are committed to a long term action, realizing that their struggle is a life-long commitment that will include advances and roadblocks throughout the way. Additionally, it is difficult to illuminate inequities within the sociohistorical contexts in which they occur. However, in doing so, ethic of critique leaders create a greater moral consciousness about indignities and dehumanization, and lay the groundwork for action that can serve to limit social inequities.

One strategy for challenging the status quo is disrupting the dominant narratives occurring within social institutions. This can be done by providing a space for silenced voices to be heard and listened to. When this occurs, the dominant narrative is countered with an alternative perspective (often one that is rarely if ever heard, (Shapiro & Stefkovich, 2005). Providing an outlet for silenced voices involves empowering marginalized communities to become agents of change, through formal and informal paths. For example, many community colleges have student success advisory committees. These committees encompass membership from academic and student affairs to provide college-level recommendations for enhancing student outcomes. An ethic of critique leader would be acutely concerned with the makeup and representation on this committee. They would ask which individual(s) or group(s) are not at the decision-making table. For instance, they may want to ensure greater representation among campus affiliates (e.g., faculty, staff, administration, and students) and by their characteristics (e.g., race, gender, etc.). A primary concern would be how those not present would become further marginalized by their lack of inclusion.

SOCIAL JUSTICE

An ethic of critique is associated with a social justice orientation. Understanding marginality and challenging domination results in action designed to transform colleges into more equitable institutions. An ethic of critique leader perceives the scope of their social justice efforts as all encompassing. They consider critical action for issues on the micro- (individual), meso- (group, organizational), macro- (societal), and mega- (cross-cultural) levels (Langlois & Begley, 2005). The aim of this critical action is to create community colleges that foster greater outcomes and opportunities for all. Thus, an ethic of critique is not designed to destroy social institutions, but to transform them into better institutions (Murray, 2009).

Table 6.2 presents some strategies that the authors of this text have seen employed by critical leaders. Given critical leaders goal of identifying inequities, we offer suggestions for data-gathering. For example, college leaders can employ wrap-sessions with faculty, staff, and or students to bring together stakeholders to discuss timely issues. These sessions can be open for dialogue on any topic or can be thematically driven (e.g., tenure process concerns, hiring diverse faculty, barriers to student success). Campus leaders can also engage in walk-through sessions where they literally 'walk' on campus, meet with students and/or staff to get to know them better. This informal strategy allows for insight into challenges to emerge organically through observation and casual conversation. The next column illustrates some domains where the information derived from such inquiries can be highlighted. One common area for highlighting challenges are professional development activities where campus affiliates (e.g., faculty, staff, administration) are shown data on inequities and asked to reflect on institutional issues that foster such inequities. The third column indicates social justice action steps that can be taken, through formal policy processes, which can lead to change. Often, change in bureaucratic organizations is motivated by lawsuits and litigious action. However, critical leaders also engage in hiring of individuals with similar perceptions and strategically situate those individuals on campus committees, initiatives,

TABLE 6.2. Critical Strategies for Creating Equity-Oriented Institutions

How inequities are identified	Domains in which evidence is shown	Indirect action steps for change	Direct action steps for change
• Needs assessment • Outcomes assessment • Surveys & questionnaires • Wrap-sessions • Walk-throughs • Testimonials and anecdotes • Informants & confidants	• Professional development • Town-hall meetings • Social media • Convocations • Committee meetings	• Recruiting and hiring critically-oriented personnel • Stacking committees with critically-oriented personnel • Changing policies to be equity-oriented • Changing accepted organizational language • Securing external support from local leaders • Lawsuits/litigation	• Sit-ins • Protests • Strikes • Marching • Petitions

and other leadership areas. Finally, the last column indicates direct action steps that can be taken, when the strategies in the third column do not culminate in desired goals. Direct action includes sit-ins, protests, and other action steps that fall outside the normal bounds of leadership. It is important to note that critical leaders are usually not visibly involved in organizing direct action; rather, they work behind the scenes to guide ("unofficially") direct action efforts.

When engaging in social justice, critical leaders must be concerned about *'trading inequities.'* This notion is derived from the work of Shapiro and Hassinger (2007), who noted that ethic of critique leaders must be cognizant that in fighting one inequity, they do not inadvertently exchange that inequity for another. They provide an example of a curricular change that requires additional focus on mathematics and reading, while reducing an emphasis on the arts and social sciences. The change itself was designed to actualize equity for marginalized student communities, but furthered their marginalizing by eliminating arts curriculum that they tended to have less access to. The preparation of these marginalized students may, therefore, be remedied in one area, but negatively affected in another, which could have ramifications for their education at higher levels. Another concern for ethic of critique leaders is *'subset advantage.'* This term refers to a circumstance where an effort to create parity aids one subgroup of a marginalized group, while not addressing the needs of the remaining members of that group (see Messina, 2006). Advantaging one marginalized subset without addressing the needs of another can foster a climate of discord and disunity among oppressed groups. Critical leaders are aware of the historical use of this divide and conquer approach in maintaining power over marginalized groups. Critical leaders 'call out' this 'divide and conquer' strategy. For critical leaders, social gains should be made as part of a comprehensive plan for action; otherwise, inequities will persist.

An ethic of critique employs a comprehensive framework to understand, illuminate, and redefine social institutions. When encountering ethical quandaries, the following questions can guide decision-making for critical leaders.

• What rule of law governs the quandary? Who created the rules?
• What groups are advantaged or disadvantaged?
• What are the interests of those at the decision-making table?
• How do the rules reify social structures and hierarchy?
• What voices are/were absent from the decision-making table?

The next section describes the benefits associated for leaders who ascribe to an ethic of critique paradigm.

BENEFITS OF AN ETHIC OF CRITIQUE

The ethic of critique serves as a counter-paradigm to traditional justice-oriented approaches to leadership. There are four important benefits that can be derived from the critique paradigm.

1. An ethic of critique upholds the rights and interests of historically disadvantaged and underserved individuals. This framework protects the interests of the powerless while challenging assumptions, biases, norms, and practices that advantage the powerful. From a cultural perspective on morality, advocating for the interests of those who lack the power and voice to do so is widely seen as a moral enterprise (i.e., the right thing to do).

2. The decision-making style provides a platform for democratic ideals to be actualized. By bringing multiple stakeholders to the decision-making table and elevating silence voices, liberty for all individuals within an organization (not just a select few) is actualized.

3. With greater representation in organizational decision-making (e.g., committees, initiatives, faculty senate, etc.), campuses can make better decisions that take into account a more fuller range of considerations, perspectives, realities, and outcomes. From a Hegelian perspective, the synthesis (the byproduct of the thesis and anti-thesis) results in the greatest argument; as such, the ethic of critique provides a counter to a traditional ethic of justice perspectives, thereby fostering better decisions. As such, respectful criticism can create healthier, more productive organizations. Students can benefit from this enhanced decision-making in a number of ways. For instance, elevated voices allows for new insights to be shared regarding student success that can create better programs, policies, and practices that benefit the underserved. Moreover, employing a critical paradigm demonstrates the value of diversity, thus, better modeling expected behaviors that students must illustrate in an increasing global multicultural workplace.

4. As a result of the aforementioned, organizations may experience tension around issues of disagreement; however, that discord can lead to greater dialogue, understanding, mutual respect and (in some cases) camaraderie.

Given the benefits of an ethic of critique, we suggest some basic steps leaders can take to become better ethic of critique leaders.

DEVELOPING A CRITIQUE ORIENTATION

Leaders can employ a number of strategies to enhance their use of an ethic of critique. Here, we discuss several potential strategies:

1. Firstly, leaders can begin employing an ethic of critique by identifying issues of inequity in their organization. The critical leader must develop their understanding of the nuances and intricacies of societal barriers. One strategy for this involves conducting needs assessments with students or staff in order to identify barriers to inclusion and success in the

college setting. Given that student success is often a topic of increasing concern among leaders, a critical leader could request college-level data from institutional research on student participation and outcomes (e.g., persistence, achievement, attainment, transfer, etc.), rates disaggregated by race/ethnicity, gender, class, disability, etc. Using this data, areas of unequal participation or outcomes could be identified; thereby serving as fodder for future discussions that explain why inequalities are evident. A similar approach could be taken by academic department leaders, using such information to identify gatekeeper courses and gatekeeper faculty. Moreover, many community colleges participate in organizational-level assessments and benchmarking, such as the Community College Survey of Student Engagement (CCSSE, McClenney, 2007). Such data, when disaggregated, could serve to illuminate areas of faculty-student engagement, campus service usage, diversity experiences, and campus climate where students have differential experiences and outcomes.

Additionally, many community colleges have become increasingly concerned about disparate outcomes for male students of color. A critical leader could use information derived from the Community College Survey of Men (CCSM), a needs assessment tool, to identify potential challenges facing male students as disaggregated by racial/ethnic affiliation (see Wood & Harris, 2013). Any assessment should be accompanied with qualitative data, specifically, the voices of the underserved. Additionally, in developing one's awareness of inequities, leaders can make it a point to engage in conversations on and off campus with varied student and staff groups. For example, college leaders can do campus walk-throughs to learn about staff members' perceptions of the campus environment. Gaining insight on various experiences and inequities requires establishing connections and relationships with staff ranging from janitors, and groundskeepers, to executive assistants.

2. Leaders desiring to develop a critical leadership frame should engage in critical reflection regarding their own biases, assumptions, experiences, and perceptions. For example, leaders should constantly ask themselves questions such as: Why am I engaging in this practice? What do I really believe is occurring in this setting? How do I feel about this particular student, staff, or faculty group? What am I assuming or taking for granted? Individuals engage in introspection in different ways. While some individuals will prefer to journal or memo, others will simply prefer finding a quiet moment to engage in introspection. Regardless of approach, the goal is to develop an ability to interrogate oneself as a strategy for becoming more aware of how one's own contribution to marginality.

3. Leaders can also consider reading works (e.g., books, journal articles, op-eds, etc.) by critical theorists. Developing a critical lens involves understanding how the multiplicity of marginality is manifested in different

contexts. As noted by Bohman (2005) many 'critical theories' (e.g., critical legal studies, critical race theory, LatCrit, TribCrit, post-colonialism, feminism, etc.) have been developed in theoretical lineage to critical theory. Bolstered by historical and contemporary social movements, these theories extend across numerous disciplines and have different marginalized groups as the center of their inquiry and action. By regularly reading works from critical authors, leaders can become more astute at naming marginality, questioning practices, and understanding the scope of injustice in bureaucratic settings.

In addition to these suggested steps, leaders should become attuned to their own leadership dispositions and practice problem solving from an ethic of critique lens. This chapter provides three resources to support the reader's development of a critique-orientation. In the following section, discussion questions are provided that can enable readers to gauge their understanding of the information presented in this chapter. Readers should begin to consider their own beliefs in relation to this chapter's content. At the end of this chapter, the Nevarez & Wood (2013) *Ethic of Critique Leadership Inventory* is presented. Use this inventory to learn more about your own leadership preferences. This inventory will provide you information needed to begin the process of critical introspection of your own actions, behaviors, and mores. Then, use the case study presented at the end of this chapter to practice addressing problems from an ethic of critique lens.

DISCUSSION QUESTIONS

1. What are the primary thematic trends in critical theory? How do these trends relate to an ethic of critique?
2. In what ways (if at all) do community colleges perpetuate social stratification? In policy? In language? In practice? In curriculum? In student programming and services?
3. How can college leaders turn school sites into emancipatory sites?
4. This chapter provided some benefits to an ethic of critique leadership approach. Do you believe there are additional benefits to this paradigm? If so, what are they? Moreover, what are the weaknesses (if any) of an ethic of critique paradigm?
5. Based on your reading of this chapter, what are some questions that you can ask yourself when approaching a dilemma from an ethic of critique lens?

DEFINITIONS

Assumption of Oppression: refers to criticalists' core belief that oppression and subjugation are inherent in the human social condition.

Base: refers to economic systems and the interrelations among divergent economic systems.

Consequentialist: meaning that the *consequences* of outcomes or byproducts of a given decision are of primary concern.

Critical Enlightenment: refers to critical theorists foci on illuminating power interests and relations in society

Critical Theory: a school of thought driven by the aim "to liberate human beings from the circumstances that enslave them" (Horkheimer, 1982, p. 244).

Ethic of Critique is a decision-making lens which is critical of societal inequities and is committed to uncovering, challenging, and overcoming inequities through social justice.

Multiplicity of Marginality: meaning that oppression is manifested, takes different forms, and evolves in different ways across different contexts

Social Justice: refers to critical theorists' commitment to emancipating and empowering society's oppressed.

Subset Advantage: refers to a circumstance where an effort to create parity aids one subgroup of a marginalized group, while not addressing the needs of the remaining members of that group.

Superstructure: is the social structure that exists on this base, including: government, social institutions, laws and codes, social relations, culture, and the arts.

Trading Inequities: refers to inadvertently exchanging one inequity for another in an attempt to create parity in a given area.

NEVAREZ & WOOD: ETHIC OF CRITIQUE LEADERSHIP
INVENTORY (NW- ECLI)

This leadership inventory is designed to aid leaders in assessing their use of ethical leadership theory. Ethical leaders strive to make the 'right' decisions; however, perspectives on the method(s) of reaching the 'right' decision can differ. While there are a number of differing ethical paradigms, this inventory focuses on the ethic of critique. Current leaders should reflect on actions that they typically take and perceptions that they hold. Aspiring leaders should consider the actions that they would take if they held a formal leadership position within an organization. Read the following statements and mark the appropriate response. If you find statements difficult to answer, trust your instinct and judgment in selecting the most appropriate response. Remember that there are no right or wrong answers:

	Strongly Disagree (1 pt)	Disagree (2 pts)	Somewhat Disagree (3 pts)	Somewhat Agree (4 pts)	Agree (5 pts)	Strongly Agree (6 pts)
1. Rules and policies often create unintended consequences for the disadvantaged.						
2. Advocating for individuals not at the "decision-making" table is my top priority.						
3. Social structures and the rules that support them perpetuate stratification.						
4. I always consider how policies can disadvantage others.						
5. Sometimes, you must ignore policies to do what is 'right.'						
6. I have a commitment to overcoming injustice.						
8. I am able to identify inequalities that others do not see.						
9. I lead to represent the voices of the underserved.						
10. I advocate against injustice.						
12. Laws are made to subjugate the powerless.						

Note: This inventory is printed with permission from the Nevarez-Wood Community College Leadership Institute. All rights reserved.

Scoring

To score your responses, do the following: add up the total sum of your responses for all of the questions in the inventory. This is your total ethic of critique leadership score. Higher scores indicated greater levels of critique orientation. In contrast, lower scores indicate lower levels of critique orientation. The maximum score possible is 60.

_____*Total Critique Leadership Score*

SCORE MEANING

While the maximum score is 60, many leaders may desire to understand their usage of this framework in comparison to other leaders. To facilitate this interest, scores from prior inventory participants were divided into percentile ranges. These percentile ranges allow leaders to understand their score in relation to other leaders. The percentile ranges are as follows: Low critique orientation (33rd percentile or lower); Medium critique orientation (34th to 66th percentile), and High critique orientation (67th to 99th percentile).

- Low critique orientation: 10 to 43 points
- Medium critique orientation: 44 to 50 points
- High critique orientation: 51 to 60 points

Total score should be contextualized in light of scores gathered from additional ethical inventories in this volume. In doing so, leaders are provided with a more accurate depiction of their ethical standing across the four primary paradigms. Ideally, equivalent orientations scores (medium, high) across all paradigms depict a well-balanced orientation. Consistency of orientation levels across the four paradigms reflects leaders' ability to be multi-oriented and multi-skilled in using ethical paradigms to effectively engage in leadership and organizational decision-making.

RELIABILITY

Two internal consistency estimates were employed to examine the reliability of the critique leadership inventory: split-half coefficient and coefficient alpha. For the split half reliability, the scale was divided into equal halves for item equivalency. We took into account the order of the measures; thus, the sequence of items was rotated. One half included items 1, 3, 5, 7, and 9, while the second half included items 2, 4, 6, 8, and 10. The split-half coefficient was .70 while the coefficient alpha was .75. Both procedures illustrated satisfactory reliability.

SUGGESTED CITATION

Nevarez, C., & Wood, J. L. (2013). *Nevarez & Wood—Ethic of Critique leadership inventory (NW- ECLI)*. Sacramento, CA: Nevarez-Wood Community College Leadership Institute.

NOTE

In the validation sample for this inventory, ethic of critique scores were positively correlated with leaders' positive self-assessment of their teamwork, problem-solving skills, and insightfulness. Ethic of critique total scores had a negative correlation with ethic of justice scores ($r = -.48$); however, a positive correlation was evident with an ethic of community ($r = .45$) and ethic of care ($r = .63$). A shorter version of the ethic of critique inventory is published as a scale in Nevarez, Wood, and Penrose (2013) *Leadership Theory and the Community College*. Stylus Publication.

CHAPTER 7

THE ETHIC OF CARE

This chapter discusses Gilligan's articulation of care-based morality in reshaping conceptions of moral development. The ethic of care leadership style is articulated as an outgrowth of Gilligan's work. The chapter overviews four primary inextricably interlinked aspects of an ethic of care, including care and compassion, community, uplifting others, and relationships. The benefits of an ethic of care leadership approach and suggestion for developing a care-based orientation are discussed.

When reading this chapter, consider the following questions:

- What was the primary conclusion from Gilligan's research?
- What are the stages of care-based moral reasoning?
- What is an ethic of care? What are the tenants that underscore the ethic of care?
- What are the strengths and limitations of an ethic of care?
- In what way (if any) can this framework enhance your leadership and inform institutional change?

GILLIGAN VS. KOHLBERG:
PERSPECTIVES OF MORAL DEVELOPMENT

Care based ethics have their most foundational articulation in moral psychology from Carol Gilligan's *In a Different Voice* published in 1982 by the Harvard Uni-

---

Ethical Leadership and the Community College: Paradigms, Decision-Making, and Praxis, pages 85–100.

versity Press. Gilligan was a student of Lawrence Kohlberg, having even done research and teaching with him. Kohlberg's theory of moral development served as the mainstay for research on moral decision-making; however, Gilligan's book would challenge the foundational assumptions of Kohlberg's research. To understand the significance of her work, we first begin with an articulation of Kohlberg's model of moral development.

Kohlberg (1980, 1981, 2008) articulated a six stage model of moral development, divided into three levels of moral reasoning, pre-conventional, conventional, and post-conventional. In the pre-conventional level, morality has an external locus to the individual. In this stage, individuals are primarily self-oriented. In the first stage, moral actions are guided by rules and authority figures with good actions being motivated by the desire to avoid punishments or receive rewards. In the second stage, morality is guided by self-interest. Individuals' actions are based on the leveraging of relationships to secure their interests and needs. In the conventional stage, individuals' transition from self-interest to otherness associated with their families and communities. They are motivated by a desire to gain approval from others. In stage three, individuals seek to be perceived as 'good' or 'nice,' therefore, their actions are designed to secure such approval. In stage four, adherence to social norms and authority are valued in context of one's relationship to society.

In the post-conventional stage, internalization of moral values ensues, with a focus on one's duty to universal rules that go beyond one's immediate socio-familial context. In stage five, laws are perceived as part of social contracts, but can be violated when greater good is produced. In stage six, principles of ethics are self-determined which are logical, universal, and consistent. Kohlberg (1973) emphasizes that these principles focus on concepts of justice and rights, "at heart, these are universal principles of *justice,* of the *reciprocity* and *equality* of human *rights,* and of respect for the dignity of human beings as *individual* persons" (p. 632, emphasis in original). In fact, he even evokes comparisons to Rawl's notion of justice and the veil of ignorance. Thus, Kohlberg's model is a justice-oriented model, which extols a justice orientation as the highest level of moral development. Feeling a disconnect with this perspective on moral reasoning, Gilligan (1982) articulated the weakness of Kohlberg's stage model. Gilligan's research suggested that girls and women engage moral reasoning in a different way than boys and men (Gilligan, 1977; Goldberg, 2000). Moreover, she noted that his theory emphasized western values of individualism and justice as the rule of law (Blum, 1988; Woolfolk, 2008). She also critiqued the moral decision-making literature, noting that the primary developmental theories were constructed by male researchers who, in some cases, used solely male populations to make normative generalizations about all individuals (Gilligan, 1995).

Noddings (2003) has noted that this research has produced a patriarchal perspective on moral reasoning which prioritizes absolutism and justice over virtues of compassion, understanding, and trust. According to Gilligan (1995) the latter values emphasize a sense of connectedness with others; while the patriarchal approach to moral reasoning esteems *disconnection,* an inner division between moral reasoning and self. Moreover, a "patriarchal social order depends for its regeneration on a disconnection" (p. 123). Gilligan (1982) noted that females are socialized to hold different values than males, with an emphasis on relationships, caring, and nurturing (in essence, an ethic of care). As a result, in Kohlberg's research, girls and women were often assessed as having lower moral intelligence than men, given that male values predominated Kohlberg's framework. In other words, girls and women were often depicted as being morally and developmentally inferior (Gilligan, 1982). With this in mind, Gilligan extended that "emotion, cognition, and action" are intertwined, "not readily separable" (Blum, 1988, p. 476).

For Gilligan, universal principles for decision-making removed the personal aspect of morality. Thus, she extended that the right course of action within a given circumstance was context specific. As such, the 'right' course of action is unique to an individual, not necessarily a universal maxim that is good for another in the same circumstance (Blum, 1988). Guided by this notion, Gilligan extended a different perspective on moral reasoning, referred to as an ethic of care. Gilligan (1995) noted that there are two primary forms of an ethic of care, a feminine ethic of care and a feminist ethic of care, the latter of which she prioritized. A *feminine ethic of care* is characterized by a moral duty to others through interpersonal relationships. These relationships esteem denial of self and otherness; "premised on an opposition between relationships and self-development" (p. 122). A feminine ethic of care is said to be practiced (or to typify the essence of one's being) in a patriarchal world, where disconnection, justice, and moral autonomy are valued. Feminine care is simultaneously expected of women by a patriarchal social order while also being devalued by the same social order. A *feminist ethic of care* also emphasizes personal connection with others as essential and foundational to life. In this ethic, the disconnection between moral reasoning and self is eliminated, the relational private world is valued, and the people's interconnection and bounding to one another is recognized. Further, while feminist care acknowledges the existence of a patriarchal social order, it is "the voice of the resistance" against this order (p. 123). Doing so requires elevating voices that are silenced and recognizing the importance of connection with others.

In addition, Gilligan notes that "a feminist ethic of care repudiates a feminist ethic of care on the grounds that a feminine ethic of care rests on a faulty notion of relationship" (p. 125). In feminine care, the transition from girlhood to womanhood is associated with selflessness. This selflessness is structured around notions of care which involve a woman's denial of self, loss of voice, and restriction of personal vitality. A feminist ethic of care does not structure care around selflessness but otherness, empowerment, and the advancement of personal vitality. Key to Gilligan's work is the notion that an ethic of care has two core components, relationships and responsibility. Personal relationships are seen as a vital aspect of morality. These relationships affirm the notion that the human social order is composed of interpersonal interlinkages. Responsibility is seen as a result of these interlinkages. Human connectedness necessitates devotion, understanding, and responsiveness to others; the latter, is an enactment of responsibility that follows relational ties (Blum, 1988).

Gilligan's and Kohlberg's models of moral development are depicted in Table 7.1. In some ways, there are similarities at the early stages of the models. For example, Kohlberg's pre-conventional stage can be said to be typified by an egocentric morality. Likewise, Gilligan's (1977) first stage notes that moral development begins at an orientation to individual survival. This is a self-focused stage where an individual person "is the sole object of concern" (p. 493). In this stage, moral actions are motivated by personal interests, benefits, and a concern for survival. Similar to Kohlberg's articulation, these concerns are fueled by an awareness of rewards and punishments for right- and wrong-doing. Gilligan articulates transitional stages between each level of moral advancement. The transition from level 1 to level 2 is marked by a shift from selfishness to responsibility. During this transition, a woman's connectedness to others envelops her with a responsibility to care for them. She notes that an example of this transition can be seen when a woman becomes a mother and has to care for her children in physically and emotionally due to the child's relational dependence on the mother. This transition leads to level 2, goodness as self-sacrifice. In this level, responsibility towards others predominates a woman's thinking. Morality is driven by societal norms and a sense of membership in the social realm. However, in this stage, "goodness [as] the overriding concern" leads to dependency on others for validation and acceptance (p. 496). A similarity is seen with this stage and Kohlberg's level 2, stage 3 on interpersonal concordance where morality is pursued through a desire to be perceived as a 'good' or 'nice' person to others. The transition from level 2 to level 3 in Gilligan's model is described as a shift from goodness to truth. During the transition, women begin to consider their own needs, desires, interests, and negotiate the degree to which they believe concern for self is moral. As such,

TABLE 7.1. Gilligan's and Kohlberg's Model of Moral Development

	Kohlberg's Model	Gilligan's Model
Level 1	Egocentric Morality	Orientation to Individual Survival
	Punishment and obedience Instrumental-relativist	Transition: Selfishness to responsibility
Level 2	Socially Normed Morality	Goodness as Self-Sacrifice
	Interpersonal concordance Law and order	Transition: Goodness to Truth
Level 3	Principled Morality	Morality of Nonviolence
	Social-contract legalistic Universal-ethical principle	

inner judgment of oneself starts to balance against outward judgments of one's actions. The final level in Gilligan's model evidences the greatest departure from Kohlberg's model. Gilligan's level 3, referred to as the morality of nonviolence, illustrates a reconciliation between responsibility to others and a responsibility to oneself. This level is referred to as the morality of nonviolence since an "injunction against hurting" is increased "to a principle governing all moral judgment and action, she is able to assert a moral equality between self and other" (p. 504). Thus, one no longer does violence to oneself in being solely other focused, recognizing that esteeming oneself is a path to personal vitality and enhanced relational wellbeing. Given this, an ethic of care prioritizes care for oneself and others, a relationship and social responsibility as the highest level of moral development, a clear contrast with a justice orientation. This notion of self versus others is explored more in the next section.

SELFISHNESS VERSUS OTHERNESS

While the ethic of care prioritizes otherness as an important ethical imperative, this orientation is not without philosophical contentions. For instance, Ayn Rand's work on self-interest espouses an alternative perception on otherness. In the 1950s and 1960s Rand argued that self-interest (not otherness) should be the basis for morality. Best known for her novel *Atlas Shrugged* and her ethical treatise *The Virtue of Selfishness* (1961), Rand was from a school of thought referred to as ethical egoism (described by Rand as objectivist ethics). *Ethical egoism* is the perspective that acting in self-interest is a moral imperative. Rand suggests that selfishness should be perceived as a virtue (a highly esteemed value), not a nefarious character trait. She noted that there was a need for a moral code which situates self-interest as the essence of morality. Moreover, she noted that the actor should always be the beneficiary of their own moral actions (self-interest). *Atlas Shrugged* is a dystopian novel about rebuilding society after it has fallen into ruin. The protagonist in the novel, Galt, makes a number of arguments that articulate Rand's ethics. He states that personal fulfillment is the sole moral purpose of life. Thus, giving to and helping others should only be done when there is a benefit for doing so. In particular, Galt states that: As a basic step of self-esteem, learn to treat as the mark of a cannibal any man's *demand* for your help. To demand it is to claim that your life is *his* property- and loathsome as such claim might be, there's something still more loathsome: your agreement. Do you ask if it's every proper to help another man? No—if he claims it as his right or as a moral duty that you owe him. Yes—if such is your own desire based on your own selfish pleasure in the value of his person and his struggle" (Rand, 1959, p. 391). Rand's articulation of ethics exists in stark contrast to that of Gilligan's notion of care. Inevitably, at some points in time, individuals will face challenges in whether personal priority supersedes that of the interests of others. At one point of another, leaders will hear others say "I had to do what I had to do at the time", "It's not what I wanted to do, but I have a family and bills" "I wanted to, but my career was on the line". At some point, self-interest is important to consider, but leaders must wrestle with where the line of self-interest ends.

Research from Eva Skoe lends some light to this challenge. The ethic of care has been undergirded by an extensive body of research, particularly from Skoe who has extended a model of moral development based on Gilligan's articulation of an ethic of care. Skoe employs a moral development measure which she calls the 'ethic of care interview.' During an interview, participants are provided with three scenarios dealing with abortion, marital fidelity, and caring for a parent. Participants are then asked to describe how they would approach resolving the dilemmas. They are then rated on a three level model of moral development. Level one, referred to as self-oriented is typified by selfishness. In this level, one is oriented only to their personal needs. As one gains an awareness to others, they begin to develop an obligatory commitment to the wellbeing of others (this is referred to as level 1.5). Level 2, other-oriented, entails an individual being altruistic, to the point of placing the concerns of others before their own. This altruism can even occur to the point of their own detriment. As an individual transition to the next level, they begin to understand that balance between others and oneself is needed (this is referred to as level 2.5). At level 3, the balance has become negotiated, with a healthy equilibrium between otherness and self. This occurs due to an understanding of the importance of one's own welfare as important to relationships with others (Pratt, Skoe, & Arnold, 2004; Skoe, 2010; Skoe et al., 2002; Skoe & Marcia, 1991).

The ethic of care interview illustrates that, while self-interest is important, otherness should be esteemed. This provides a *clear departure* from Rand's work which sees otherness as beneficial only if there is a personal interest and benefit in doing so. As evident, the linkage between an ethic of care interview and the moral development stages espoused by Gilligan is clear. Research using this approach has found several findings worthy of note. Firstly, an ethic of care has been showed to be associated with positive identity development, volunteerism, charitable donations, and enhanced cognitive functioning (Helkama, 2004; Juujärvi, 2006; Skoe, 1998). Moreover, women have been found to exhibit higher levels of care (particularly in the areas of sympathy and empathy) in comparison to men (Skoe, 2010). Now, this does not mean that men do not illustrate care; however, Gilligan "conceptualizes the ethic of care as a gendered construct, beginning with the premise that women see and experience the world differently from men" (Enomoto, 1997, p. 352). Thus, men do illustrate an ethic of care (to varying degrees); however, they are generally socialized towards a 'justice' paradigm.

The notion of an ethic of care has been extended beyond the literature in moral psychology to the field of leadership studies. The result has been an articulation of a care-based approach to leading organizations that emphasizes relationships and social responsibility (Furman, 2003). With this in mind, the next section articulates an ethic of care.

THE ETHIC OF CARE DEFINED

An ethic of care is derived from the writings of scholars such as Carol Gilligan, Nel Noddings, and Eva Skoe (among many others). As a leadership and decision-making framework, an ethic of care emphasizes the social interconnectedness between leaders and followers and vice versa. The *ethic of care* is defined as a decision-making paradigm that prioritizes virtues of care, compassion, trust, and understanding. Similar to the ethic of critique paradigm, the ethic of care is juxtaposed to an ethic of justice. Specifically, ethic of care leaders are consequentialist decision-makers (Caldwell, Shapiro, & Gross, 2007), meaning that they are concerned with the consequences of personal (e.g., actions, behaviors), and professional (e.g., policies, procedures, processes) decisions. Their concern is centered on the need to affirm and empower others through a lens of care and otherness (Gilligan, 1982; Noddings, 2003). Leaders employing this lens are attentive to the needs of individuals and groups, focusing on hearing and reflecting upon their interests and making decisions that treats others with respect, dignity, and compassion (Shapiro & Stefkovich, 2005).

Noddings (2008) noted that an ethic of care, like an ethic of justice, is obligatory. In other words, leaders have a moral obligation to do right. Noddings refers to this as "a sense that I must" (p. 291). However, while an ethic of justice leaders' obligation is upholding the rule of law, an ethic of care leaders' obligation is to others. She notes that, for an ethic of care leader, a moral obligation is best expressed as a moral inclination—which she perceives as bearing greater internal duty than professional obligations. This otherness typifies an ethic of care. These leaders have a moral inclination to care for others, respond to their needs, and love them. Across the literature, the authors perceive four primary inextricably interlinked aspects of an ethic of care that are evident: care and compassion, community, uplifting others, and relationships. Using these elements as a framework, we provide context to the core principles of an ethic of care.

Ethic of care leaders are exemplified by care and compassion. These virtues (highly esteem values) guide their leadership, interactions, decision-making, and advocacy. When approaching decisions, ethic of care leaders are concerned with how the outcome will be perceived by others and make them feel. Caring for others necessitates that leaders want the best for them. Thus, an ethic of care leader values others goals, dreams, and aspirations. This care supersedes the workplace context, focused on the whole individual (personal and professional). Such leaders are also concerned with followers' satisfaction and happiness. Thus, they truly care and do their best to support followers as they navigate personal and professional challenges, pitfalls, and setbacks. Care requires an emotional connection and trust between leader and follower. Noddings (2008) notes that in some circumstances, ethic of care leaders will encounter people with whom they do not want to express care to. She states that this can occur for a variety of reasons, including an individual being unfriendly or disagreeable, having an exhaustingly large need, or oven exhaustion resulting from an output of care. In such circum-

TABLE 7.2.   Ethic of Care Components, Core Virtues and Leadership Benefits

Primary leadership styles	Democratic
Focus of ethical standard	Consequentialist (ends)
Frame of Reference	Otherness
Objective	Prioritizing relationships
Key Values/Virtues	Care, compassion, and trust
Theoretical Underpinning(s)	Gilligan's writings on Moral Development
Primary Question	How do I best express care and concern?
Core Principles	1. Care and Compassion 2. Community 3. Uplifting Others 4. Relationships
Leadership Benefits	1. Develops buy-in though inclusivity 2. Greater organizational commitment 3. Enhanced follower self-efficacy 4. Positive work climate 5. Enhanced team-based decision-making Care and Compassion

stances, she states that leaders must recall past experiences where they were cared for or cared for others, and use that inspiration to reclaim their moral inclination to care. This does not mean that ethic of care leaders should be 'trampled' by otherness. As with the ethic of care interview, a balance is made between otherness and individual needs.

COMMUNITY

Conveying care and compassion for others occurs at both the individual and environmental level. Climates of harmony are manifested by care leaders. Developing, maintaining, and growing a sense of community is a core priority of care-based leadership. Ethic of care leaders foster environments that are typified by mutual understanding, trust, shared concern, and love. Departments and organizations are viewed as familial domains. Honest discourse can only be fostered and embraced in safe environments where one is not concerned how the information shared with another will be used for advantage. Moreover, the tone of conversation among and between leaders and followers is focused on seeking common ground. As with any family, this does not suggest that individuals would or should always agree, but that disagreement is done in a caring manner where others opinions and being are valued. A core element of developing community requires involving others in decision-making. In fact, decision-making processes as a whole value individual and group input, and are reflective of how actions and decisions made will influence the community atmosphere. Caring leaders embrace community-building, encouraging formal and informal get-togethers. If a leader perceives that an individual or group is slowly drifting from the community, effort is made through informal mechanisms (e.g., coffee, lunch) to draw that person back in. If a follower has a success, the caring leader expresses their gratitude to the follower in a manner which affirms the individual success and conveys appreciation to other individuals (e.g., "Hey all, Sarah just received a grant to fund a mentoring program for underserved students. I am so honored to work with all of you; you are such a stellar team." The purpose of this two-fold message is to ensure that the celebration of one success does not create discord, combative competition, or envy; but builds up all individuals. This notion of uplifting others is explored more in the next section.

UPLIFTING OTHERS

One important aspect of an ethic of care is uplifting others. This occurs through affirmation of people's abilities, and investment in their personal development. An ethic of care leader must express confidence in others and reassure individuals of their abilities. Noddings (2008) notes that confirmation is an important aspect of an ethic of care. Ethic of care leaders make it a point to tell their followers that they are valued, admired, and essential. Affirmation for ethic of care leaders is an authentic enterprise. When a follower does well, even in small matters, the leader conveys their appreciation through verbal communication (e.g., "great work," "thank you so much," "this is fantastic," "I appreciate you so much," "what would we do without you"?) and non-verbal body language. As an authentic enterprise, affirmation must be rooted in reality; otherwise it will be received as insincere by the followers and their colleagues. As such, building up others does not suggest that leaders be blind to workplace missteps and/or moral failings. When a workplace mistake is made, the leader identifies it and addresses it. However, the manner in which this is done is what separates ethic of care leaders from other leaders. Corrections are done in a manner that maintains the followers trust, dignity, and illustrates a true interest in their personal and professional well-being. With regard to moral failings, when an individual commits a transgression against another, the leader should identify the concern and communicate that they "believe the act is not a full reflection of the one who committed it" (Noddings, 2008, p 298). Throughout this process, the leader must illustrate their care in a way which connects with others.

RELATIONSHIPS

Ethic of care leaders are committed to personal relationships with other. Their locus and investment of time and energies is in the private domain. Jos and Hines (1993) note that ethic of care leaders are concerned with in-person interactions where the parameters of the relationship are not predetermined by the authority of the post or generalized to all individuals. Rather, relationships evolve over time based on the unique intricacies of the relational dynamic. Being consequentialist in nature, this organic mode of operation prioritizes people as focused on the private outgrowths or byproducts of the relationship as opposed to viewing the relationship as a means to an end (such as in an ethic of justice). Noddings (2008) noted that dialogue is a pre-requisite for care. It is a primary strategy used to demonstrate care in relationships. Dialogue involves two aspects, speaking to others and hearing from others. Both of these aspects are essential; otherwise the communication can be perceived solely as "talking at" or "eliciting." In building and maintaining relationships, carers must be attuned to whether their demonstration of care is being received as such. A caring leader conveys confidence in others' strengths, takes time with others to recollect on past experiences, does not shy or avoid away from jovial conversation, inquires on others wellbeing, and demonstrates concern for the welfare of others. Thus, dialogue is centered on the individual, not solely on professional responsibilities. Noddings (2008) notes that an ethic of care requires that leaders understand what decisions will be best for all people. Thus, during decision-making, socially responsible leaders make judgments based on individuals and outcomes that are best for individuals, as well as others affected by or connected to the individual. Noddings notes that socially responsible leaders "ask 'what are you going through? Before we act, as we act, and after we act, it is our way of being in relation" (p. 297).

An ethic of care leader employs a comprehensive framework to understand, build trust, and convey care for others. When encountering ethical quandaries, the following questions can guide decision-making for caring leaders.

- How will this decision impact others? How will it make them feel?
- Does this decision convey care and compassion?
- What message will be communicated by this decision? Does that message convey trust and mutual understanding?
- How can I best express (i.e., through language, disposition, action) my care for others in this circumstance?
- Which course of action would best help others in this situation?
- How will this influence our sense of community?

The next section describes the benefits associated for leaders who ascribe to an ethic of care paradigm.

BENEFITS FOR AN ETHIC OF CARE

There are a number of benefits that are derived from an ethic of care leadership style. Firstly, care-based leadership develops buy-in through inclusivity. By ensuring that all members of the team of cared for, valued, and affirmed, the followers feel more included in organizational processes. Often, the byproduct of inclusivity is a deeper level of buy-in and enhanced productivity. Secondly, enhanced buy-in leads to greater organizational commitment. Followers who are committed to an organization or leader will 'go beyond the call of duty.' In doing so, they will work harder and longer because they are committed to their work and the vitality of the institution. Moreover, organizational commitment can reduce turnover, ensuring that 'good' followers continue to be dedicated to the vision and mission of the organization. Thirdly, as noted throughout this chapter, ethic of care leaders affirm those around them. Authentic affirmation invariably leads to enhanced follower self-efficacy (confidence in their ability to perform and execute tasks). Increase confidence means that the leader can begin to trust followers with greater levels of responsibility, thereby reducing the workload of the leader and increasing the efficiency of the overall unit. Fourthly, a focus on otherness creates a positive work climate. Ethic of care leaders foster work climates where there are greater levels of satisfaction. Satisfaction is an essential necessity for enhanced focus and directed attention to tasks. Fifthly, an ethic of care leader elicits feedback from individuals and groups on decision-making. They do so because they are interested in how decisions made will impact others. By eliciting feedback, enhanced team-based decision-making occurs where more perspectives lead to better and more informed decisions.

DEVELOPING AN ETHIC OF CARE ORIENTATION

While an ethic of care emanates from feminist ethicians, it should be noted that they do not believe that care is an innately feminine disposition. Rather, they suggest that, as a generalization, women are socialized to care while men are socialized to be emotionally stoic (Noddings, 2008). Thus, *some* men may need to work harder to develop an ethic of care orientation. Ethic of care leaders are engaged in personal relationships with others. Thus, to be an ethic of care leader you must first 'like people.' This is an essential building block for this decision-making paradigm. It is important to recognize that a 'healthy' care for others requires a 'healthy' care for oneself. Leaders who can't balance their own personal and professional lives (particularly those who are overcommitted to the profession) will have difficulty in being attuned to the needs of others. Care based leadership requires individuals being centered. Often, centering is a result of health familial connections and spiritual development. Balance, itself, is a process that is sought after, an ongoing struggle between the demands of the profession and personal commitments.

Ethic of care leaders must possess a high degree of socio-emotional intelligence. In fact, Gilligan notes that the concept of socio-emotional intelligence is an outgrowth of her work. *Emotional intelligence* refers to one's own awareness of their feelings, assumptions, and dispositions. *Social intelligence* refers to one's awareness of others feelings, assumptions, and dispositions. Taken together, leaders with a high degree of socio-emotional intelligence understand their emotions, can pick up on the emotions of others, and have an adept understanding of social cues. With regard to the latter, leaders with socio-emotional intelligence understand how their actions, behaviors, and dispositions are being interpreted by others around them. With this in mind, we define *socio-emotional intelligence* as an adept awareness of social cues as they relate to one's own emotions and that of others. Developing socio-emotional intelligence is a difficult process. It requires a significant degree of introspection about one's own processes, carefully watching how others act and react to interpersonal interactions, and being honest in asking trusted colleagues for feedback on whether or not they are correctly interpreting communication (verbal and nonverbal) from others.

According to Noddings (2008), developing an ethic of care requires reflection, "not only should we reflect on our competence as carers, but we can now also consider our role as models" (p. 294). Thus, college leaders who want to exemplify a care-based style should take time to reflect on the needs of their followers. Being attuned to their needs requires a clearer understanding of follower dispositions, goals, and motivations. An example of this is provided by Noddings (2008). She provides an illustration of a teacher who, for the best interests of her students is very strict. She notes that serving as a model for care in some cases means modifying one's behavior to demonstrate love and compassion for the purpose of moral education. She notes that an ethic of care necessitates that a carer must "be engrossed in the cared-for, and the cared-for must receive the carer's efforts as caring" (p. 294). As part of a reflective practice, ethic of care leaders should approach decision-making with concern for others, their feelings, and the interests of organizational community.

As made evident above, developing a care-based leadership style requires leaders to personally interact with their colleagues. Interaction requires speaking with others about personal and professional matters. This does not mean that leaders should overexpose themselves, but rather, view relational development as a gradual process. When interacting with others, leaders should make it a point to tell them that they are valued. This should occur regularly. Hearing from others is also an important component of an ethic of care. Leaders can develop their caring orientation by asking others how they are doing. When doing so, leaders should be authentically interested in the response and being fully and emotionally present during the conversation. Leaders should strive to empathize with others, not just to sympathize. In all, prioritizing the personal and private world over the official and public world should be the ideal.

While this chapter has outlined some steps that leaders can take to develop an ethic of care orientation, these steps are merely a starting point. To further your development, the following section outlines discussion questions that allow readers to engage in critical introspection on their own care-oriented assumptions, practices, dispositions, and behaviors. Following this is the presentation of a case study that allows leaders to engage in real-life dilemmas, and determine how the issues presented can be resolved through a care-based lens. Remember to 'get inside the theory' and envelop yourself in the mores, principles, and considerations of an ethic of care leader. After resolving the case from this perspective, then, other lenses can also be considered. This chapter also features, the Nevarez

& Wood (2013) *Ethic of Care Leadership Inventory*. This inventory is designed to facilitate leaders' assessment of their ethical tendencies and propensities as it relates to an ethic of care. Use the scores from the inventory to better understand your leadership in context of care. As a whole, the discussion questions, case study, and inventory serve as the next step in your understanding and use of an ethic of care lens.

DISCUSSION QUESTIONS

1. How does Gilligan's perspective on moral development differ from that of Kohlbergs? In what ways do these perspectives influence leadership styles and approaches?
2. In what ways do you ascribe to an ethic of care orientation?
3. What are some areas (e.g., care and compassion, community, uplifting others, relationships) of an ethic of care orientation that you can improve on?
4. Identify three leaders in your organization who you respect. In what way, if any, do they demonstrate an ethic of care?
5. How would you describe your balance between being self-centered and other-centered?
6. What are the benefits of an ethic of care paradigm? In what ways, do you believe an ethic of care paradigm may have weaknesses?
7. Based on your reading of this chapter, what are some questions that you can ask yourself when approaching a dilemma from an ethic of care lens?

DEFINITIONS

Disconnection: an inner division between moral reasoning and self.

Ethic of Care: a decision-making paradigm that prioritizes virtues of care, compassion, trust, and understanding.

Ethical egoism: the perspective that acting in self-interest is a moral imperative.

Emotional Intelligence: refers to one's own awareness of their feelings, assumptions, and dispositions.

Feminine Ethic of Care: is characterized by a moral duty to others through interpersonal relationships.

Feminist Ethic of Care: emphasizes personal connection with others as essential and foundational to life, but eliminates the disconnection between moral reasoning and self.

Socio-Emotional Intelligence: an adept awareness of social cues as they relate to one's own emotions and that of others.

Social Intelligence: refers to one's awareness of others feelings, assumptions, and dispositions.

NEVAREZ & WOOD: ETHIC OF CARE LEADERSHIP INVENTORY (NW- ECLI)

This leadership inventory is designed to aid leaders in assessing their use of ethical leadership theory. Ethical leaders strive to make the 'right' decisions; however, perspectives on the method(s) of reaching the 'right' decision can differ. While there are a number of differing ethical paradigms, this inventory focuses on the ethic of care. Current leaders should reflect on actions that they typically take and perceptions that they hold. Aspiring leaders should consider the actions that they would take if they held a formal leadership position within an organization. Read the following statements and mark the appropriate response. If you find statements difficult to answer, trust your instinct and judgment in selecting the most appropriate response. Remember that there are no right or wrong answers:

	Strongly Disagree (1 pt)	Disagree (2 pts)	Somewhat Disagree (3 pts)	Somewhat Agree (4 pts)	Agree (5 pts)	Strongly Agree (6 pts)
1. Care and compassion typify my leadership style.						
2. Creating a sense of community at work is an ethical imperative.						
3. My chief concern is the well-being and welfare of my staff.						
4. Workplace relationships must be typified by trust and understanding.						
5. To be effective, a leader must care about and affirm their staff.						
6. I prefer/enjoy investing in the personal and professional development of my staff...						
7. I enjoy community-building at work.						
8. I value the experience, insight, and knowledge of my staff.						
9. I spend time building a family-like atmosphere at work.						
10. I believe that building a sense of community is vital to organizational success.						

Note: This inventory is printed with permission from the Nevarez-Wood Community College Leadership Institute. All rights reserved.

Scoring

To score your responses, do the following: add up the total sum of your responses for all of the questions in the inventory. This is your total ethic of care leadership score. Higher scores indicated greater levels of care orientation. In contrast, lower scores indicate lower levels of care orientation. The maximum score possible is 60.

_____*Total Care Leadership Score*

SCORE MEANING

While the maximum score is 60, many leaders may desire to understand their usage of this framework in comparison to other leaders. To facilitate this interest, scores from prior inventory participants were divided into percentile ranges. These percentile ranges allow leaders to understand their score in relation to other leaders. The percentile ranges are as follows: Low care orientation (33rd percentile or lower); Medium care orientation (34th to 66th percentile), and High care orientation (67th to 99th percentile).

- Low care orientation: 10 to 48 points
- Medium care orientation: 49 to 53 points
- High care orientation: 54 to 60 points

Total score should be contextualized in light of scores gathered from additional ethical inventories in this volume. In doing so, leaders are provided with a more accurate depiction of their ethical standing across the four primary paradigms. Ideally, equivalent orientations scores (medium, high) across all paradigms depict a well-balanced orientation. Consistency of orientation levels across the four paradigms reflects leaders' ability to be multi-oriented and multi-skilled in using ethical paradigms to effectively engage in leadership and organizational decision-making.

RELIABILITY

Two internal consistency estimates were employed to examine the reliability of the care leadership inventory: split-half coefficient and coefficient alpha. For the split half reliability, the scale was divided into equal halves for item equivalency. We took into account the order of the measures; thus, the sequence of items was rotated. One half included items 1, 3, 5, 7, and 9, while the second half included items 2, 4, 6, 8, and 10. The split-half coefficient was .93 while the coefficient alpha was .86. Both procedures illustrated satisfactory reliability.

SUGGESTED CITATION

Nevarez, C., & Wood, J. L. (2013). *Nevarez & Wood—Ethic of Care leadership inventory (NW- ECLI)*. Sacramento, CA: Nevarez-Wood Community College Leadership Institute.

NOTE

In the validation sample for this inventory, ethic of care scores were positively correlated with leaders positive self-assessment of their social abilities. Ethic of care total scores had a positive correlation with ethic of critique ($r=.63$) and ethic of local community ($r=.62$) scores. A shorter version of the ethic of care inventory is published as a scale in Nevarez, Wood, and Penrose (2013) *Leadership Theory and the Community College*. Stylus Publication.

CHAPTER 8

THE ETHIC OF LOCAL COMMUNITY

This chapter examines the moral philosophy of utilitarianism as articulated by Jeremy Bentham and John Stuart Mill. The authors also discuss the concept of communitarianism. Drawing upon these two frameworks, the ethic of local community is discussed as a neo-utilitarian and communitarian approach for decision making. This framework, specifically designed for community college leaders, places the focus of decision-making on the best interests and needs of the local community served by the institution.

When reading this chapter, consider the following questions:

- What is utilitarianism? How is it defined?
- Do acts or rules take predominance in determining the consequences of a decision?
- What are the strengths or limitations of an ethic of local community?
- In what way (if any) can this framework enhance your leadership?

This chapter begins with an overview and discussion of the core concepts in utilitarianism and communitarianism. These moral philosophies undergird the ethic of local community.

Ethical Leadership and the Community College: Paradigms, Decision-Making, and Praxis, pages 101–116.

UTILITARIANISM

Utilitarianism is an ethical framework derived from the writings of Jeremy Bentham and John Stuart Mill. These philosophers believed the best actions were those which reduced pain and increased pleasure. This perspective places best interests of society (or the community) above those of the individual, seeking to create a better society for all (Beckner, 2004; Strike, 2007; Sucher, 2008; van Staveren, 2007). Utilitarianism is commonly associated with the phraseology 'the greatest happiness' principle or 'the greatest good for the greatest number.' Mill (1863/2003) indicated that "utility, or the Greatest Happiness Principle, holds that actions are right in proportion in as they tend to promote happiness, wrong as they tend to produce the reverse of happiness. By happiness is intended pleasure, and the absence of pain" (p. 143). Thus, Mill suggests that the best course of action in a given circumstance serves to reduce pain and enhance pleasure. In contemporary ethics, pleasure is equated with the general welfare and pain with harm. As a result, 'just' actions are connected to the outcomes or effects of those actions for the general public good. Thus, the consequences of decisions bear greater importance than the mechanisms or 'objective' standards by which they are made. For instance, from a utilitarian perspective, "an action is not right or wrong simply because it is a case of telling the truth or lying; and the moral rule against lying is not, in itself, correct. Lying is wrong because, in general, it has bad consequences" (West, 2004, p. 1). Indeed, a utilitarian would suggest that some circumstances demand aberrations from truth in order to avoid catastrophic consequences (e.g., murder, genocide, robbery).

Early utilitarian's were chiefly concerned about social reform (e.g., women's rights, workers' rights, voting rights) (West, 2004). They had a strong interest in changing laws that were either perceived as meaningless or exploitative. In particular, they believed that laws which tended to produce unhappiness as opposed to happiness were not 'good' laws. Such laws were 'unjust' laws as they lacked social utility. Moreover, they noted that many policies are context-laden, meaning that they are connected to socio-historical contexts. However, Bentham stated that contexts are in flux, thus he noted that as social contexts change, social policies should also change with these contexts (Driver, 2009).

Bentham also recognized that the nuances of maximizing pleasure and reducing pain could lead to different interpretations of the right course of action. As a result, he extended seven decision-making considerations that, when faced with an ethical quandary, could assist in determining the most appropriate action (Driver, 2009). These considerations included: a) intensity—the strength of the good to the drawbacks (or pain) produced; b) duration—the length of the pleasure produced by the a potential course of action; c) certainty—the degree that one is confident that the decision made will manifest good (pleasure); d) proximity—the time lapse between the act and the pleasure derived from the act; e) fecundity—the likelihood that the action will result in further benefits or drawbacks; f) purity—the degree of overlap in the action producing both pleasure and pain; and g) extent—the total population to be impacted by the action (Bentham, 1789).

Of course, employing such as wide array of considerations is only beneficial for large-scale decisions; every action could not be subject to such an expansive array of considerations. As such, Bentham argued that experience could serve as a bellwether for moral deliberations in uncomplicated matters.

Utilitarianism has had an important impact on public policy. For example, public policy often uses cost-benefit assessments to determine what the right course of action is in policy-making. In doing so, the goal of maximizing 'welfare' while reducing 'harm' are pursued. This approach has its roots in utilitarian ideology, where welfare and harm are merely proxies for pleasure and pain (Bowen, 2005; West, 2004). As noted by Dupré (2007), Bentham perceived that such a rational approach to decision-making that avoided making decisions based on typical moral inclinations resulted in better moral and social decisions. In fact, Bentham even extended the notion of *'felicific calculus'*, a quantitative process where actions were measured based on a predetermined rubric for pleasure and pain; and the right course of action was determined by higher scores for pleasure after subtracting pain.

Mills did not accept this quantitative approach to moral decision-making, believing that ethical decisions required qualitative insights as well. He stated, "It is quite compatible with the principle of utility to recognize the fact, that some kinds of pleasure are more desirable and more valuable than others. It would be absurd that while, in estimating all other things, quality is considered as well as quantity, the estimation of pleasures should be supposed to depend on quantity alone" (Mills, 1863/2003, p. 144). While Bentham viewed pleasures (irrespective of type) as equivalent in nature, Mills espoused a hierarchy among pleasures. He suggested that pleasures could be categorized on distinct levels. Mills placed intellectual and aesthetic pleasures over social or physical enjoyments. In arguing this point, he noted that "there is no know…theory of life which does not assign to the pleasures of the intellect, of the feelings, and imagination, and of the moral sentiments, a much higher value as pleasures than to those of mere sensation" (p. 144). Mills further noted that Utilitarianism views mental pleasures as being superior to bodily pleasures in that they facilitate greater "permanency, safety, [and] uncostliness" (p. 144). He also suggested that maximizing pleasure, in some instances, could require a delay of gratification. However, he noted that long term pleasures could be perceived as bearing greater utility over time than short term pleasures.

There are two very different interpretations of Utilitarianism as espoused by Bentham and Mills. The first is act utilitarianism. *Act utilitarianism* holds that the maximization of utility should be considered for all acts, each time an ethical quandary is encountered. The second form is *rule utilitarianism*, which maintains that rules should be made which *tend* to maximize utility; these rules are then followed as principles which guide individual acts (Dupré, 2007; Wilson, 2007). Typically, discerning which rules promote utility is based on past experiences and cases (Bowen, 2005). For example, act utilitarianism would suggest that dismissing a quality administrator who one knows is wrongly to blame for a deleterious accreditation result, in some instances, could result in greater organizational wellbeing. Thus, an act utilitarian could, in pursuit of greater utility, concur that dismissing the employee is the correct action. However, a rule utilitarian could suggest that, as a rule, dismissing quality administrators who are unjustly blamed for poor organizational outcomes does not promote the general welfare, despite beneficial consequences for organizational morale. Thus, a rule utilitarian could conclude that such a dismissal would be wrong.

One challenge associated with a utilitarian approach is determining what the scope of greater utility should entail. To advocate for the 'greatest good' suggests that a common frame of reference exists for which to base one's advocacy (Nevarez, Wood & Penrose, 2013). For example, Ciulla (2003) notes that utilitarianism multiplies happiness in the interest of the "majority of stakeholders: in an organization, a community, or a country" (p. 143). For a leader, greater clarity is needed on the scope of interest, as Nevarez et al., (2013) note that college leaders could interpret utilitarianism to refer to a county, region, state, national, or the globe. Addressing this point, in the context of an ethic of local community, requires some discussion on communitarianism.

COMMUNITARIANISM

Communitarianism is a philosophical perspective (most associated with political philosophy) which places the community as the focal point for all value judgments. In other words, the advancement of the community serves as the primary concern. Community advancement is all encompassing, inclusive of local culture, social dynamics, common practices, belief systems, and history (Etzioni, 2003). Thus, discussing common characteristics of communitarian principles are difficult, as community interests are situational and context-laden. Bell (2010) best clarified this focus by noting the communitarians perceive the community as the 'standard of morality.' In this light, all rights and privileges originate from the community (Noddings, 2003). As such, standards of right and wrong are viewed as emanating from the community itself; with no pre-established bounds of justice predating the community. In this light, communitarianism is, to some degree, community-based relativism (Wood & Hilton, 2012).

Communitarianism is a relational philosophy; it is relational in that the lives, experiences, realities, and outcomes for people in a given community are viewed as interdependent. Thus, an action taken by one member of the community has important implications and ramifications for other members of the community. Moreover, in order to maintain social order, communitarians believe that individual community members must all have roles within the community and carry out those roles. In essence, the community is a social system, where one member can cause disruption, thereby jeopardizing the strength and continuity of the entire system (Wood & Hilton, 2012).

Like utilitarianism, one challenge associated with communitarianism is determining the scope of its focus. More specifically, placing the community at the center of moral decisions has limited utility when there is disagreement on what is and is not within the bounds of the communal social system. Thus, Etzioni (2003) has noted that communitarian scholars have focused on defining parameters that demarcate a community. In contributing to this line of inquiry, Etzioni suggests that there are two primary elements that are characteristic of a community. Firstly, communities are constituted of 'affect-laden' relationships among individuals. Secondly, communities are composed of shared commitments to beliefs, customs, traditions, and identity. Clearly, this definition allows for a wide interpretation of community.

Community colleges are influenced by communitarian values. Historical and contemporary scholarship on community colleges has routinely affirmed the importance of this community-oriented focus of community colleges (Baker, Dudziak, & Tyler, 1994; Bogue, 1950; Cohen, 2001; Cohen & Brawer, 2003; Eells, 1931, 1941; Mills, 2003; Monroe, 1977; Vaughan, 2006). Unlike other institutions of higher education, the community college is specifically designed to serve the needs of the local community, hence the word 'community' in the name 'community college' (Bogue, 1950; Nevarez & Wood, 2010; Vaughan, 2006).

Correspondingly, most community colleges were established at the local level. In the early days of community colleges, this often meant that the local community literally fundraised and built the campus (Ratcliff, 1994). If a community identified having an educational center as a need, then a local college was built. Eventually, colleges were developed as a response to state-level needs, but the origins of community colleges were based on local community needs (Cohen, 2001). For example, Fresno Junior College was established in 1910 as the first community college in California. Cohen and Brawer (2003) noted that the justification provided for the establishment of the college was that "there was no institution of higher education within nearly two hundred miles of the city" (p. 19). Thus, the institution was established to fulfill local educational needs to a region that was isolated (due to proximity) from educational opportunities.

It should be noted that prior to 1947, community colleges were referred to as junior colleges in order to emphasize their focus on general education as opposed to advanced (or senior) major studies (Cohen & Brawer, 2003). However, in that year, the Truman Commission on Higher Education released a national report highlighting the valued role that junior colleges have in serving the needs of the local communities in which they are imbedded. To illustrate this point, the report used the term 'community' college to indicate that junior colleges serve localized needs and are often overseen by local councils and boards (Gleazer, 1994; Medsker, 1960; Vaughan, 1983). The popularity of this term has grown with importance over the years, resulting in the American Association of Junior Colleges (the leading association of community colleges) to be renamed the American Association of Community and Junior Colleges and late (more simply) the American Association of Community Colleges (AACC, 2009). With the aforementioned context on utilitarianism and communitarianism, the next section defines and delineates the core components of an ethic of local community.

ETHIC OF LOCAL COMMUNITY DEFINED

The *ethic of local community* is a decision-making paradigm which grounds the right course of action in the best interests and needs of the local community. This ethic, articulated specifically for community college leaders, suggests that these leaders parameterize 'good' outcomes to focus on their local service regions. Using this paradigm, the local community serves as the framework for decision-making (Nevarez et al., 2013); as such, the chief value in decision-making is the strength and success of the local community (Nevarez & Wood, 2012). How success is operationalized is dependent upon local community needs, but typical domains of interest include social, cultural, political, economic, as well as human and intellectual capital needs (Wood & Hilton, 2012). The ethic of local community is a consequentialist paradigm. It is consequentialist in that the *consequences* (or ends) of a given decision are the focal point of determining what one ought to do in a given circumstance (Northouse, 2007); this is juxtaposed to the non-consequentialist (means based) approach employed in an ethic of justice (Nevarez, Wood & Penrose, 2013).

The ethic of local community is a neo-utilitarian and communitarian framework. The ethic of local community differs from traditional utilitarianism in that the scope of the greatest good is specified. In this perspective, the greatest good is confined to the local community (or target region) for which the community college serves. Thus, the ethic of local community is more appropriately conceptualized as neo-utilitarian, as the scope of the greater utility is parameterized (Wood & Hilton, 2012). Simply put, an ethic of local community leader leads with one concern in mind, the best interest of our local community. All other considerations, even those occurring within the campus domain are secondary. The ethic of local community is communitarian in that the primary role of community colleges is to serve the best interests and needs of their local communities (Nevarez & Wood, 2012). Since its inception, community colleges have served local community needs by providing access to higher education to communities where postsecondary opportunities were elusive (Cohen & Brawer, 2003). These institutions feature educational programming designed to develop and foster local capital (e.g., social, economic, intellectual, human, cultural) needs (Vaughan, 2006). This does not mean that national and state needs are not of importance; however, they are ancillary to local needs.

Guided by utilitarianism, an ethic of local community assumes a balance between act and rule utilitarianism, with a *tendency* towards the prior. In general, leaders create rules, codes, policies, and processes that are designed (based on past experience and data) to foster the greater good for the local community served by the college. Given the shifting sociopolitical landscapes of local communities, ethic of local community leaders continually evaluate the utilitarian-guided rule of law to ensure that the general welfare exceeds that of the harm caused by such rules. When needed, an ethic of local community requires that new rules are enacted (as informed by prior cases), which serve to articulate utility-driven rules for future quandaries.

However, in many circumstances, leaders face quandaries that have no clear articulation in the rule of law, or are areas of concern that are value concerns as opposed to policy concerns. Examples of value concerns could include determining where to erect a new building, crafting program outcomes for student affairs programming, determining how much time to spend with a given constituency (e.g., faculty, students, policymakers, administration, community leaders). As a result, in such circumstances, the leader then relies upon an act utilitarian approach, making decisions in which the act itself is designed to produce the greatest good for the local community. When faced with such decisions, Bentham's (1789) seven principles (e.g., intensity, duration, certainty, proximity, fecundity, purity, and extent) can serve as context to guide decisions; though small decisions can employ experiential knowledge and rudimentary cost-benefit analyses for guidance.

There are several core principles of an ethic of local community (see Table 8.1). They include: localism, community priority, rationality, reductionism, and intellectual welfare. *Localism* refers to placing the needs and interests of the local community above that of the state (used in the broadest sense). Thus, while subject to federal, state, and regional policies, a leader employing an ethic of local community framework places primary value on the service region of the college. This approach is employed based on a belief that local decision-making will result in better outcomes for the local community than decisions made at the federal and state level. For example, Brice Harris (Chancellor of the California Community Colleges) noted that the California system is comprised on 112 colleges with 72

TABLE 8.1.   Ethic of Local Community Components, Core Principles and Leadership Benefits

Primary leadership styles	Democratic/Servant Leadership*
Focus of ethical standard	Consequentialist (ends)
Frame of Reference	Local interests
Objective	Advancing the welfare of the local region
Key Values/Virtues	Localism, civic mindedness, and the public good
Theoretical Underpinning(s)	Utilitarianism and Communitarianism
Primary Question	What is in the best interest of our service region?
Core Principles	1. Localism
	2. Community Priority
	3. Rationality
	4. Reductionism
	5. Intellectual Welfare
Leadership Benefits	1. Local Buy-in and Support
	2. Extra-organizational clarity
	3. Intra-organizational clarity
	4. Common language and messaging
	5. De-depersonalizes decision-making

Note: *This leadership approach draws elements from multiple styles.

locally elected and controlled boards of trustees. He noted that despite criticisms of the expansiveness of the trustee structure, the system is beneficial:

> although there have been numerous reports that have recommended a much more centralized system, I am convinced that any organizational efficiency achieved by that approach would be negated by the loss of local responsiveness to local educational needs"...this system is actual highly effective and, I believe, the best way to ensure that local communities have colleges that meet their local needs (Harris, 2013, p. 58).

This perspective is a clear example of localist perspective on college governance. Now, localism does not suggest that college leaders be blind or ignorant to wider societal issues and trends. Instead, community college leaders should be attuned to issues beyond that of local interest, as aligning the college with national efforts (e.g., STEM) can result in additional resources that meet the best interests of the local community. Moreover, an ethic of local community should not be perceived as isolationist. Inter-college linkages and partnerships are greatly needed to provide opportunities for local students. Thus, Wood and Hilton (2012) suggest that ethic of local community leaders should esteem college collaborations with other entities and institutions to meet the best interests of all communities. Evidence of this approach is often seen in articulation, where colleges establish partnership in the areas of curriculum, systems, and policies in order to benefit the interests of their students (and by intent, their local communities). However, united actions should not circumvent, overshadow, or take dominion over local interests and needs.

While a justice-oriented paradigm places emphasis on individual rights; utilitarianism and communitarianism view individual rights as subject to community rights. This perspective illustrates the principles of *community priority* (Wood & Hilton, 2013). Serving the needs of local communities is a complex, multifaceted aim, especially given this heterogeneous nature of communities served by community colleges. For instance, a community college may have a service region composed of diverse micro-communities, differing in locale (e.g., urban, suburban, rural), socio-economic status (e.g., low income, middle class, high income), racial/ethnic affiliation (e.g., Black, White, Latino, Asian), and other important areas of distinction. A leader guided by an ethic of local community is attuned to these nuances, and recognizes the role of the institution is serving a diverse set of local interests and needs.

In Utilitarianism, the happiness of one individual is equivalent to that of another. In other words, one person's individual good is not weighed greater or lesser than that of another (Driver, 2009). Thus the cumulative benefit of individual interests is prioritized in decision-making. The greater good does not seek to trample individual rights, but to order their importance as appropriate to the greater public good (Arthur, 1998; Beckner, 2004; Strike, 2007; Sucher, 2008). For example, Fujimoto (2012) noted that community college leaders, in their pursuit of maximizing good in difficult budget times, may determine to cut funding to programs serving smaller groups of students than those serving greater numbers. Of course, given that some equity-oriented programs are small-scale (boutique) programs; this approach when employed can result in more undesirable outcomes for some populations as opposed to others. However, this is a necessary challenge in leadership in pursuit of the best interests of the local community for whom the college serves. This is where the rational decision-making element of an ethic of local community is most evident. As noted previously, Bentham (1789) perceived that utilitarianism allowed for a departure from moral inclinations or intuition. Rather, the ethic of local community provides a consequentialist framework for making rational decisions, which can result in greater, rationally pursued outcomes for the community.

One core consideration espoused in an ethic of local community is *reductionism*, delimiting college missions and functions to those that meet the best interest of the service population. Specifically, Nevarez et al., (2013) noted that achieving the best interests of the community often requires a "reductionist view of the college's respective mission (e.g., comprehensive educational programming, open access, lifelong learning) and functions (e.g., transfer, terminal degrees, remediation)" (p. 71). The expansive mission of the community college has often forced the institution to be 'all things to all people.' External pressures from the national, state, and regional landscape only serve to complicate whose interests the college serves. However, in an era marked by declining state support, increased levels of accountability, and skyrocketing enrollments, community colleges have been required to be more efficient, effective, and relevant with evaporating resources (Nevarez & Wood, 2010). As such, in practicality, meeting the best interests and needs of local communities may require college leaders to make difficult decisions about local needs and interests. Local needs take priority in decision-making over national and state interests, except where greater interests are aligned with those of the local community. Additionally, remember that one core element of Bentham's (1789) seven principles of pleasure is *fecundity*, the likelihood that the action will result in further benefits or drawbacks. To achieve sufficient outcomes for the local community may require restricting mission and function efforts. In other words, "leaders operating from this perspective focus on obtaining excellence in a more limited number of areas that are most important to the vitality of the local community as a whole" (Nevarez et al., 2013, p. 71).

Intellectual welfare entails achieving local community needs through academic programming. While community colleges certainly have numerous resources that can aid the success of local communities (e.g., buildings, staff, equipment, parking), the primary avenue by which the best interest of the local community is obtained is through academic programming. This academic programming is derived from the multiple functions of the community college, such as: transfer, remedial education, terminal degrees, vocational training, and continuing education (Nevarez & Wood, 2010; Tillery & Deegan, 1985; Vaughan, 2006). This focus on intellectual welfare is derived from Mills notions that mental pleasures are superior to social or physical enjoyments. The role of community colleges are to advance their local communities, the tool used for this aim is academic programming. Other considerations are pursued secondarily. By placing high value on the intellectual welfare of the local community, college leaders will facilitate greater local "permanency, safety, [and] uncostliness" (Mills, 1863, p. 144).

An ethic of local community uses a neo-utilitarian and communitarian framework to make decisions in the best interest of local communities served by community colleges. Bearing this framework in mind, the following are some questions that can guide decision-making for community college leaders.

- What are the implications of potential courses of action for the local community?
- What is in the best interest of the local community?
- Do the current rules in place advance utility?
- What decision will maximize the general welfare and reduce harm?
- How will the local community interpret the decision made?

The next section describes the benefits derived from employing an ethic of local community decision-making lens.

BENEFITS OF AN ETHIC OF LOCAL COMMUNITY

There are several benefits for college leaders who employ an ethic of local community. Firstly, by being responsive to local community needs, leaders can gain greater buy-in and support from their local communities for the advancement of the institution. For example, buy-in from the business sector can result in internship, apprenticeship, and employment opportunities for graduates. Moreover, buy-in from local non-profit leaders can create service-learning opportunities for students, where they can both learn to apply course content in practical settings and give back to their local communities simultaneously. General buy-in from the local communities can also result in support for bond measures being approved by local electorates. In an era marked by dwindling local and state resourcing of colleges, such measures are essential to an institutions fiscal viability. Moreover, imbeddedness within local communities can also increase the likelihood that advancement (i.e., fundraising) campaigns will produce needed monies to support the institution.

Secondly, community colleges have numerous missions (e.g., comprehensive educational programming, open access, lifelong learning) and functions (e.g., transfer, terminal degrees, remediation) that require an endless amount of leadership considerations. For example, without a focus on localism, community college leaders are more subject to divisions on the primary scope of their service. Some leaders may place greater focus on the best interests of regional, state, national, or global needs. An ethic of local community provides extra-organizational clarity on the scope of external interests that take priority in decision-making. In this light, the local community takes priority among other extra-organizational pressures. Thus, colleges need not be reactive institutions, responding to the whimsical priorities of national or state political and economic interests; but rather, proactively focus on serving their local needs and only meeting greater needs when aligned with local interests.

Thirdly, an ethic of local community also benefits leaders by providing a focal point for rectifying intra-organizational (within college) disputes. Invariably, leaders must negotiate the numerous interests among and between administrators, faculty, staff, and students. An ethic of local community provides a framework for negotiating conflict, focused on factors external to the institution. College discourse can then shift from what a particular group wants or needs to what the local community wants or needs. Knowing that the local community is the primary population of interest in decision-making provides *service clarity*, a greater understanding of whose interests the college should serve.

Two related benefits result from enhanced intra-organizational clarity. Fourthly, service clarity results in streamlined messaging and a common language of practice within an organization that clarifies and refines organizational activities around one unified focus—the community. Fifthly, an external locus of decision-making depersonalizes decisions that are difficult to make. For example, a leader who must cut a program can then shift the focus of personal antipathy from themselves to the appropriate focus, community needs and interests. While this approach will certainly not eliminate ill will directed towards the leader on behalf of the organizational affiliates affected, it certainly can serve to partially deflect and re-center the conversation on the local community and the leader's role as a representative steward.

DEVELOPING A LOCAL COMMUNITY ORIENTATION

There are several steps that leaders can employ to better position themselves as ethic of local community leaders. Firstly, they can read literature written on utilitarianism from John Stuart Mill and Jeremy Bentham. There are numerous arguments made on behalf of this framework that are too expansive to cover in this chapter. Reading these works will provide leaders with a deeper context by which to adhere to an ethic of local community. Secondly, to advocate on the best interests of one's community, a leader must be knowledgeable of the needs of that community. As a result, leaders should seek to imbed themselves in their local communities, attending community events (e.g., fairs, town halls, parades, sporting, council meetings, industry gatherings, conferences). The goal of attending these events is to connect with a wide array of community leaders to learn about the human, intellectual, and economic capital needs of the local community. Thirdly, a related recommendation is that college leaders establish community advisory councils to provide input to inform decision-making. Advisory councils can be sector based, with separate councils for business/industry, local government, non-profit, religious, K–12 education, and other sectors. While such committees should exist at the college-level, departmental leaders in academic and student affairs can also consider having advisory councils which allow them to best understand how their efforts can be aligned with the interests of the local community.

Fourthly, another strategy for gaining insight into local issues is needs assessments. While learning about local needs from local leaders is one important aspect of informing decision-making, data should always be preferred to anecdote. As a result, college leaders should regularly engage in needs assessments in various sectors to learn what the best interests of the community are. Now, in times of limited financial resources, conducting regular assessments can be costly endeavors. In addition to institutional research staff, colleges can also provide incentives for community college faculty as well as doctoral students and faculty from local universities to assist the college in conducting needs assessments. Fifthly, while the aforementioned strategies provide insight into common community concerns, (formal and rudimentary) cost-benefit analyses should also be employed as an additional strategy to determine which actions and decisions will have the greatest positive effect on the welfare of the local community. This approach has been employed by public policy makers for some time and could have manifold benefits for community college leaders. Sixthly, as informed by local input, leaders should examine program and student learning outcomes across all departments within the institution to determine their alignment with the needs and interests of the local community. Then, outcomes based assessment can be employed to evaluative the utility of programming with two aims in mind; first, identifying whether local needs are actually being met by such programming; and second, using outcomes assessment to improve extant programming to better meet local community needs. Leaders can also consider employing Bentham's (1789) seven principles as a guide to inform assessment, evaluation, and cost-benefit processes.

In addition to the above steps, leaders should begin to consider their own beliefs as they relate to the ethic of local community espoused in this chapter. One strategy for doing this is to have greater insight into one's leadership dispositions. At the end of this chapter, the Nevarez & Wood (2013) *Ethic of Local Community Inventory* is presented. This inventory will provide readers with questions that will help them assess their leadership beliefs, perceptions, and values as it relates to an ethic of local community. Then, leaders can use the case studies presented at the end of this chapter to practice addressing problems from an ethic of local community lens.

DISCUSSION QUESTIONS

1. What is utilitarianism? What is communitarianism? How do they relate to an ethic of local community?

2. Review Bentham's seven considerations for utility (e.g., intensity, duration, certainty, proximity, fecundity, purity, and extent). Are each of these

considerations integrated into your current organizational decision-making processes? If so, how? If not, what would they add (if anything) to decision-making?

3. What is act utilitarianism? What is rule utilitarianism? As noted, an ethic of local community assumes a balance between act and rule utilitarianism, with a *tendency* towards the prior. What potential challenges may unfold in negotiating this balance?

4. This chapter provided some benefits to an ethic of local community leadership approach. Do you believe there are additional benefits to this paradigm? If so, what are they? Moreover, what are the weaknesses (if any) of an ethic of local community?

5. Based on your reading of this chapter, what are some questions that you can ask yourself when approaching a dilemma from an ethic of local community lens?

DEFINITIONS

Act Utilitarianism: a utilitarian perspective which holds that the maximization of utility should be considered for all acts, each time an ethical quandary is encountered.

Communitarianism: is a philosophical perspective which places the community as the focal point for all value judgments.

Community Priority: the perspective that community rights outweigh those of the individual.

Ethic of Local Community: a decision-making paradigm which grounds the right course of action in the best interests and needs of the local community, parameterized as the service region of the college.

Fecundity: the likelihood that the action will result in further benefits or drawbacks.

Felicific Calculus: a quantitative process where actions are determined by scoring pleasure and pain considerations.

Intellectual welfare: achieving local community needs through academic programming.

Localism: refers to placing the needs and interests of the local community above that of the state (used in the broadest sense).

Reductionism: delimiting college missions and functions to those that meet the best interest of the service population.

Rule Utilitarianism: a utilitarian perspective that maintains that rules should be made which *tend* to maximize utility; these rules are then followed as principles which guide individual acts.

Service Clarity: a greater understanding of whose interests the college should serve.

Utilitarianism: a moral philosophy which holds that the right action is one that promotes happiness and reduces pain.

NEVAREZ & WOOD: ETHIC OF LOCAL COMMUNITY
LEADERSHIP INVENTORY (NW-ELCLI)

This leadership inventory is designed to aid leaders in assessing their use of ethical leadership theory. Ethical leaders strive to make the 'right' decisions; however, perspectives on the method(s) of reaching the 'right' decision can differ. While there are a number of differing ethical paradigms, this inventory focuses on the ethic of local community. Current leaders should reflect on actions that they typically take and perceptions that they hold. Aspiring leaders should consider the actions that they would take if they held a formal leadership position within an organization. Read the following statements and mark the appropriate response. If you find statements difficult to answer, trust your instinct and judgment in selecting the most appropriate response. Remember that there are no right or wrong answers:

	Strongly Disagree (1 pt)	Disagree (2 pts)	Somewhat Disagree (3 pts)	Somewhat Agree (4 pts)	Agree (5 pts)	Strongly Agree (6 pts)
1. The cardinal mission of the community college is to serve the needs of the local community.						
2. The 'greatest good' is what benefits our local area.						
3. Meeting the needs of our service region is one of my chief concerns.						
4. I use whatever strategies and leadership styles necessary to benefit the community we serve.						
5. I consider the ramifications that decisions will have on the local community.						
6. I take time to learn about the needs and interest of our local community						
7. I advocate on behalf on the needs of my local community.						
8. The primary measure of success is whether the college is meeting the needs of the local community.						

	Strongly Disagree (1 pt)	Disagree (2 pts)	Somewhat Disagree (3 pts)	Somewhat Agree (4 pts)	Agree (5 pts)	Strongly Agree (6 pts)
9. The best interests of the local community outweighs all other considerations.						
10. Community colleges exist to serve the needs of their local communities.						

Note: This inventory is printed with permission from the Nevarez-Wood Community College Leadership Institute. All rights reserved.

Scoring

To score your responses, do the following: add up the total sum of your responses for all of the questions in the inventory. This is your total ethic of local community leadership score. Higher scores indicated greater levels of local community orientation. In contrast, lower scores indicate lower levels of local community orientation. The maximum score possible is 60.

_____ *Total Local community Leadership Score*

SCORE MEANING

While the maximum score is 60, many leaders may desire to understand their usage of this framework in comparison to other leaders. To facilitate this interest, scores from prior inventory participants were divided into percentile ranges. These percentile ranges allow leaders to understand their score in relation to other leaders. The percentile ranges are as follows: Low local community orientation (33rd percentile or lower); Medium local community orientation (34th to 66th percentile), and High local community orientation (67th to 99th percentile).

- Low local community orientation: 10 to 44 points
- Medium local community orientation: 45 to 52 points
- High local community orientation: 53 to 60 points

Total score should be contextualized in light of scores gathered from additional ethical inventories in this volume. In doing so, leaders are provided with a more accurate depiction of their ethical standing across the four primary paradigms. Ideally, equivalent orientations scores (medium, high) across all paradigms depict a well-balanced orientation. Consistency of orientation levels across the four paradigms reflects leaders' ability to be multi-oriented and multi-skilled in using ethical paradigms to effectively engage in leadership and organizational decision-making.

RELIABILITY

Two internal consistency estimates were employed to examine the reliability of the local community leadership inventory: split-half coefficient and coefficient alpha. For the split half reliability, the scale was divided into equal halves for item equivalency. We took into account the order of the measures; thus, the sequence of items was rotated. One half included items 1, 3, 5, 7, and 9, while the second half included items 2, 4, 6, 8, and 10. The split-half coefficient was .91 while the coefficient alpha was .86. Both procedures illustrated satisfactory reliability.

SUGGESTED CITATION

Ethic of local community total scores had a positive correlation with ethic of critique scores ($r = .45$) and ethic of care scores ($r = .62$). Nevarez, C., & Wood, J. L. (2013). *Nevarez & Wood—Ethic of Local community leadership inventory (NW- ELCLI)*. Sacramento, CA: Nevarez-Wood Community College Leadership Institute.

PART III

PROBLEM-SOLVING THROUGH CASE STUDIES

CASE STUDY 1

ACCESS IS NOT ENOUGH

A Case on Peer Mentoring

Paige E. Sindt

Metro Phoenix Community College (MPCC), an urban commuter campus located in downtown Phoenix, Arizona, is one of the state's largest postsecondary education and career training institutions in Arizona. MPCC has approximately 12,000 students pursuing certificate and degree programs for career training and advancement, lifelong learning, or preparing for transfer to a four-year institution. MPCC is a designated Hispanic Serving Institution, enrolling one of the largest Hispanic college student populations in the nation.

BACKGROUND

A major ten year strategic planning initiative led by the President's Office released in 2000 created a campus vision that shifted the institutional focus from access to retention. As a result of the "Access is not Enough" initiative, an institutional Retention Committee, comprised of ten rotating faculty and staff from various academic and service units (two year appointments), was tasked with increasing fall to fall student retention rates for first-year certificate and degree seeking stu-

Ethical Leadership and the Community College: Paradigms, Decision-Making, and Praxis,
pages 119–125.
Copyright © 2014 by Information Age Publishing

dents at MPCC. While retention improved as a result of the Retention Committee interventions during the 2000–2010 timeframe, it fell short of the ten-year goal. As such, upon review of preliminary 2011 retention data, the President's Office charged the Retention Committee with a new plan seeking to improve student retention by approximately 11 percentage points, from 62% to 73% over a three-year period, reaching the retention goal by 2015. Upon reviewing the last five years of retention data, the committee determined that they must focus outreach efforts toward traditional age students (18–21), as institutional data suggest the sharpest decline in retention occurs in this group. Disproportionate attrition levels among first-generation, minority and students of immigrant parents were evident. This was especially important, since this was the largest student population at the institution.

Upon review, the committee examined available campus support services and learned that the Office of Academic Affairs currently provided students access to tutoring, advising, and general learning support, such as writing tutoring, along with various academic success skills workshops and seminars. Based upon research in increasing retention, the committee determined these resources to be among the most effective tools needed for early intervention. To better understand the available resources, usage, and campus climate to support these services, the committee convened a series of faculty and student focus groups. Results showed low usage in critical areas, such as math and writing tutoring, suggesting a disconnection in students' knowledge of these available services or a lack of comfort in seeking out or utilizing available services.

Focus group meetings demonstrated, and institutional data corroborated, that, while underutilized, the campus offered strong resources and reputable programs. The retention committee focused attention on addressing the disconnection in student awareness, comfort, and perception of the multiple learning support resources available. A psychology faculty member on the Retention committee, Dr. Lucia Ryder, suggested that the institution consider developing a formal student mentoring program. Dr. Ryder has experience with a similar program from her previous institution, California State University, Northridge (CSUN), which was highly successful. CSUN research demonstrated that peer mentoring is the "single most important factor associated with high retention and graduation rates for low-income, first-generation college students" (CSUN EOP Director, José Luis Vargas, personal communication, March 2011). Dr. Ryder proposed that a similar peer mentor program could be designed to bridge the gap, connecting students with key institutional resources, and providing role models as well as creating more student leadership opportunities on campus. Participants would have access to a network of peer leaders, engage in more campus activities, and utilize support services. Foundational research about student persistence (Astin, 1977, 1993; Tinto, 1987), suggested retention is significantly impacted by the level and quality of peer interactions, leading to students' ability to integrate into the campus community.

The committee agreed with Dr. Ryder's recommendation and determined that the directive of creating a formal peer mentoring program should be the responsibility of the Office of Student Affairs (OSA), as they oversee similar initiatives related to student engagement and leadership on campus. The retention committee sent their recommendation to the President of MPCC, who approved the committee's suggestion. OSA was notified late in the summer with a timeline for implementation for the following spring semester. The President wanted the committee to begin a pilot program, hone the program policies and structure, and then rigorously expand the program to the entire student population. While none of the Student Affairs staff were on the retention committee, they were informed that this was an institutional directive to improve retention, and a key directive of the President, for which OSA and the retention committee will be held accountable. OSA was directed to report progress via bi-annual reports to the retention committee and the President's office. In turn, the retention committee will determine the effectiveness of the program in addressing persistence concerns by comparing the number of mentoring participants and a similar group of non-participants after the program has been in place for two terms.

In the Office of Student Affairs, recent departmental re-organizations created serious concerns for existing staff about the job security and the department's future. In the previous academic year, the offices of Student Leadership Programs and Student Affairs were combined, resulting in two colleagues being laid off, and another individual resigned as a result. None of these positions were replaced, leaving two full-time staff and one part-time administrative support to manage the day-to-day departmental responsibilities. The OSA team was supervised by a busy Director who also had oversight of four other critical campus departments. While committed to supporting students, after budget cuts and being denied additional staffing lines to manage numerous programs and initiatives, the remaining Student Affairs staff felt overwhelmed and under-supported by their Director and institution at large. This led to a perception that the value of the department is minimal on campus, and there was a general sense of low morale pervading the office.

When the OSA staff received the directive to create a new peer mentoring program for the spring semester from the retention committee, they were frustrated again by the demanding roles, lack of support, and unrealistic expectations. They also believed they should have been consulted when making decisions about creating the program, as they believe it should have been housed in Academic Affairs. The OSA staff felt strongly about this and they approached their Director, but he disagreed and told them this was the President's directive, OSA will take the lead and be held accountable. Accordingly, OSA staff developed a peer mentoring program, following the CSUN model combined with a nationally cited model of best practices developed by Colorado State University (CSU). CSU's program was designed for incoming freshmen, pairing a first-year student with a junior or senior student who participated in a semester of training prior to serving as a mentor. CSU Mentors typically lived on campus, with or near their mentees, to build community and encourage involvement in CSU student life. Each mentor was also assigned a faculty or staff advisor and a group of 5–25 participants based on an interest, passion, or identity.

Given OSA's many responsibilities and limited resources, they implemented the program, but staff had a hard time recruiting mentors and participants, making time to train and support mentors, and lacked time to make any programmatic adjustments to better fit the four-year CSU model to the community college setting. Further, given the best practices model employed was implemented at a four-year residential campus, structural changes for a two-year commuter institution complicated the application of the model. During the first semester, four students volunteered as mentors. The staff held an evening four-hour training meeting with the mentors, but due to scheduling conflicts, not all mentors participated in the training. A total of six participants signed up for the program in the first semester it was offered. Only two continued with the program throughout the semester. Mentors were given the flexibility to structure the program themselves and were asked to report back to OSA staff, though OSA staff had little time to give them feedback or monitor their activities. The following semester, the staff was hopeful that interest will grow, but ended up with only two mentors and five participants. After one year of implementation, OSA reported to the retention committee and the President's Office that the peer mentoring program should be discontinued due to lack of student interest. OSA cited student feedback of participants, as well as resistance from Academic Affairs as they perceive the program to be threatening to the academic support services they already offer.

The retention committee disagreed with OSA's proposal to discontinue the peer mentoring program, but was troubled by the apparent lack of student interest. Dr. Ryder, who was then the President of the Faculty Senate, suggested that a sub-committee be convened under her direction, with members from Academic Affairs, Student Affairs, and recent student participants in the program. The President tasked his special assistant, Cindy Mau, with learning more about why the program did not succeed, by speaking more in depth with OSA and student participants. As part of Cindy's fact-finding initiative, she interviewed two program participants, a mentee and a mentor. The following is what she learned.

Program Mentee: Yesenia Gallegos was an 18 year-old female student in her first semester at the local community college. She planned on transferring to a nearby four-year university after completing two years at the community college. She was studying business and psychology. She was also working as a bank teller part-time every afternoon Monday through Friday. Yesenia was passing her classes with B and C grades, but found the first semester to be quite challenging and was concerned as she will be taking more difficult classes her second semester. Recently, she also learned that she will need to earn a 3.0 GPA to get into the university business program as a transfer student. Yesenia mentioned her concerns to her Psychology professor and advisor, Dr. Ryder, who told Yesenia about the new Peer Mentor Program available in the spring semester. She spoke highly of her experience serving as a faculty advisor for the peer mentors at her former institution. Yesenia decided to participate and signed up immediately to be paired with a mentor for the spring semester.

After a few weeks into the spring semester, she still had not received a mentor placement and was frustrated with the OSA office for not responding to her inquiries. About one month into her second semester, she was happy to learn she had been paired with a mentor, Ben Jansen, a second-year student, and made an appointment. On the day of their meeting, Ben showed up late and seemed unprepared for their meeting. Yesenia wasn't sure what to expect, but she cautiously told Ben she was nervous about passing classes, and was considering withdrawing from some of her math and psychology classes. Ben was friendly, but he seemed uncomfortable and wasn't able to provide any specific suggestions.

After the second, equally unproductive meeting, she decided not to participate any longer and stopped going to their appointments. Seeing Ben on campus shortly after missing a recent appointment, she tried to avoid him, but he intercepted her, surprising her with an apology, saying he felt unprepared to be a mentor and wasn't sure what he was supposed to do or say in his role, especially when she told him she was considering dropping out of classes. Yesenia did schedule an appointment with the writing center and found the resources helpful for writing assignments for her intensive psychology courses. The support was critical in helping her decide to stay enrolled for the semester.

Program Mentor: Ben Jansen was in his second year, and was preparing to transfer to a four-year degree program. Ben held a 3.75 GPA, and was studying business and communications. He had taken almost all of the courses he needed and had free time during his last semester at MPCC. He was encouraged by his advisor to consider participating in a new mentoring program to strengthen his resumé and help with his application to transfer into the university business program. Ben decided to volunteer, though he was disappointed to learn that he would not receive any academic credit, and there were no other incentives to participate, other than as a resumé-enhancing activity.

Training was scheduled a few weeks into the semester with little notice. During training, OSA staff showed up late and not all the mentors are there, even though Ben was told that the training was mandatory, requiring him to take a night off work. OSA staff quickly reviewed what it meant to be a peer mentor, stressing the importance that mentors listen and provide support to their mentees, but should not overstep boundaries and counsel their peers. The staff shared the model from Colorado State University on which MPCC's program was designed, but Ben struggled to see how the programs were similar given CSU's mentors took a semester long class about mentoring, earning credit, and they lived on campus with their mentees.

During break, Ben overheard the staff talking about their frustrations with the program and the retention committee. Ben gathered it was an important institutional initiative and becomes nervous about his role. His first mentee, Yesenia, asked for his advice whether she should drop her classes or not. Ben hesitated in responding as he did not want Yesenia to take his advice to stay in class and then be upset with him if she did poorly in her classes, nor did he want to encourage her to drop out of classes. He felt that either way, he would disappoint his mentee or the OSA staff. After the disastrous meeting, he tried to schedule a meeting with OSA staff to ask them what he should have done, but they weren't available when he stopped by their office on several occasions. He met with Yesenia again, this time suggesting that she speak with the OSA staff directly. Yesenia did not show up to their next two scheduled appointments. Shortly after, he saw her on campus and decided to apologize to her for not being more helpful. He invited her to get together for a casual social event, where he found it easy to tell her about similar struggles he experienced in balancing work and school, and he suggested she visit the writing center, about which she had not yet known. Ben completed the semester as a mentor, but was dissatisfied. He wanted to be honest about his experience with OSA, but he was hoping for a letter of recommendation, so when they asked him his thoughts about the program, he declined to provide specific feedback.

DISCUSSION QUESTIONS

1. What are the central issues and key leadership theories applicable to this case?
2. What critical assumptions and decisions did the Retention Committee use or ignore that may have led to a different outcome with regard to the following:
   a. The relation of retention and leadership.
   b. The role of Academic Affairs and existing student learning support services on campus.
   c. Dr. Lucia Ryder and her experience with peer mentoring.
3. Is the Office of Student Affairs at fault for the lack of success of the first year of the Peer Mentoring Program? Why or why not? What issues prevented the program from being successful from a theoretical standpoint? Discuss the following:
   a. What examples did the staff use to develop the program model? Was this an effective model? Why/why not?
   b. Describe any parallels between the dysfunctional organizational leadership the staff themselves were experiencing and the peer mentoring leadership program they created. How do they relate? How do they differ?
4. An effective peer mentor, by definition, is a knowledgeable ally and role model who is a good listener and communicator. Mentees must trust their peer leaders. Discuss the following:
   a. Was Ben an effective peer mentor? Why or why not?

   b.   Did Yesenia achieve her goals of participation in the peer mentor program? Why or why not?

   c.   What positive and negative outcomes resulted for both the mentor and mentee as a result of participation in this program?

5.   What issues impeded the success of the program and how might those be addressed with the recommended new program model?

CASE STUDY 2

DIVERSITY, HIRING, AND THE REALITY OF HIGHER EDUCATION

John D. Harrison

BACKGROUND

As a rural community college in southern Mississippi, Wilhelm State Community College (WSCC) was faced with an opportunity to address diversity among its faculty makeup. The college employs 173 faculty members, of which five percent are member of a minority group. This is in stark contrast to the 36% of the student population who are minorities. With the accreditation visit rapidly approaching, the pressure for the college to increase faculty diversity had never been more pressing, making every decision about new hires important. It was common knowledge that the accrediting body reviews faculty diversity, and has given Areas of Improvements (AIP) to community colleges in the past. These AIPs have been known to cause issues in passing the accreditation process and were a concern for WSCC.

In order to address faculty diversity, a college-wide diversity initiative was created to increase job postings and college awareness in journals and professional organizations that reached a diverse audience. The initiative was spearheaded by

Ethical Leadership and the Community College: Paradigms, Decision-Making, and Praxis,
pages 127–131.
Copyright © 2014 by Information Age Publishing
All rights of reproduction in any form reserved.

the President of WSCC, who had a successful track record of increasing faculty diversity in her previous positions at other institutions. In order to broadcast the college's efforts, diversity awareness articles were published in the college monthly paper, and the President's annual State of the College Address focused heavily on WSCC's commitment to diversity. All search committees pursuing new faculty hires were trained in the initiative and expected to consider diversity when making final selections. Special emphases were paid to the value and benefit of diversity in the college, as well as the legal and accreditation implications of a lack of diversity among the faculty.

Tyrell Buckner, Associate Professor of Biology at WSCC, was selected to chair the Search Committee. The position had been announced three months ago with great excitement, as WSCC was seeing unprecedented growth. Given the diversity initiative, it was important that the process be viewed as fair and balanced by the college community as a whole. For this position, the candidate was to have a Masters, or higher, in biology with relevant teaching experienced, preferably at the community college level. The search was expansive, with emphases on placing job postings in journals and professional associations that would reach diverse candidates, including females, who meet or exceeded the department's criteria. Being that this was the first hire under the new diversity initiative, a great deal of attention would be focused on the process.

Scrutiny is nothing new for Tyrell. He was considered fair, balanced, and just in his demeanor and with his dealings with others. Most faculty and staff trusted and respected his decisions, feeling that he had a strong moral compass and was a person of integrity. As an African-American faculty member, he had a unique perspective on the hiring process, the culture at WSCC, and the new diversity hiring initiative. This combination of factors made him the ideal chair to lead this process.

The posting attracted a great deal of attention with the committee receiving 238 applications, interviewing 15 candidates, and selecting five for in-person interviews. From those interviews, feedback from students, faculty, and staff were collected and given weight. After a long and extensive search, the committee had narrowed the field to two potential hires, Dante and Betty. They would be announcing the decision in February. Tyrell sat down to review the Search Committee minutes for the previous week's meetings. One thing was clear; this would not be an easy decision to make.

Dante was interviewed and well received by the search committee. Fresh from a Ph.D. program, he had an accomplished academic record having taught courses as a graduate student, writing several publications, and winning the graduate teaching award at his alma mater. The recommendations from his chair, the Dean in his prior college, and several professors indicated that he was well liked by his colleagues, and his teaching evaluations spoke volumes about his ability to connect with students in the classroom. Many of the faculty members at WSCC liked Dante, having met him during the tour of the facilities. While, at 31 years old, he was much younger than the majority of the faculty, it was clear that Dante fit the requirements of the new position.

The second candidate, Betty, had a confident interview with the search committee. She was being considered for a number of reasons, and would be a much welcomed addition to the all male faculty in the department. Her accomplishments were varied and included eight years of community college teaching experience, where she was well received by students. Betty's knowledge of biology was well recognized having been developed through her Masters, and her practical experience in a hospital laboratory. At 43 years old, committee members agreed that she would be perceived as more mature and "seasoned" than Dante and this may benefit the interactions between her and the students. Having been associated with WSCC as an adjunct in the past, she was familiar with the culture and the operations of the college. Through this experience however, faculty members knew her to be arrogant with a sense of entitlement that came solely from being the daughter of the Dean of Arts and Sciences for WSCC. This left many in the faculty with reservations about her ability to be a productive member of the full-time faculty.

As he reflected on the minutes, Tyrell remembered discussions he had with other colleagues and the Dean about the hiring process, with one particular candidate in mind. It wasn't long ago that Tyrell spoke with Joe Wilson, a faculty member from the Chemistry Department. The conversation still resonated with him. "I hear you're leading the search for that new faculty opening in the Biology Department. How's that going?" Joe said. "Well, so far so good. We've had a pretty good response rate and I think we're really going to be able to find a good fit." replied Tyrell. "That's great," Joe continued, "I want you to take a look at this CV. The Dean asked me to pass it along to you. It's his daughter and she's looking for a job." Skimming it over Tyrell said, "Oh, well thanks. You know, I'll look it over, but we've already got a few candidates that I think would really add a great deal to the department and I don't know if she's right for the position." Joe replied, "Hey, I understand completely. I was asked by the Dean to pass it along and wanted to make sure that I put it in your hands. Just between you and me, do you mind if I give you a little advice? I know you're up for tenure this year. Given the fact that you've got a family to worry about and with all of your obligations, you wouldn't want to do anything to jeopardize all you've worked for. I don't envy your decision. Anyway, it's great talking to you and good luck with that search."

Since that time, Tyrell's family had been on his mind. Tyrell had made a great deal of sacrifices to get this far in his career. He had missed seeing his children during his time in graduate school, and had moved his family half way across the country to take the position at WSCC. There were many nights Tyrell spent writing papers, attending faculty functions, and working with students as opposed to going out with his wife or spending time with his children. Tenure would be the culmination of all of this hard work and give him the opportunity to finally make it up to his family. This decision could potentially impact everything he had worked so hard for these years. While the institution grants faculty due process in the tenure review, there had been several instances where the outcome in that process seemed to favor the college over the faculty member's credentials. Tyrell was left with an uneasy feeling about the residual outcomes from the committee's decision, and how this might influence his career in the future.

Continuing to dwell on discussions he had about this decision, he thought about how the Dean had stopped by to see him. "Hi Dr. Buckner, I'm glad I caught you. I understand that Dr. Wilson brought my daughter's CV by for you to look at a couple of weeks ago. I trust that you had a chance to review it," said the Dean. "He did, yes. I've taken it to the committee for review, and will be sending out correspondence soon to all of the candidates, and following up with the final candidate when the decision is made in February." "Well, that's good," said the Dean, "She's been having a tough time finding a faculty position having been away from it for so long. I trust that you'll help the committee make the *right* decision. Oh, before I go, I wanted to let you know that I received your documents for tenure. I'll be reviewing those in March. Well, have a great day!" said the Dean.

After reflecting on the conversations with Joe and the Dean, Tyrell decided to approach Dave, a friend who had come to the college at the same time as he, and who had been a confidant during the rapid growth at WSCC. Tyrell trusted Dave's opinion, as he had always been very open and honest, and had a way of cutting right to the chase. He explained the situation, hoping that Dave could provide some direction on how to proceed. "I don't know what to tell you," Dave said. "It sound's like you've got a tough decision to make. Which way are you leaning?" Tyrell replied, "Well, Dante is a great fit for the position, but it *is* the Dean's daughter and I'm up for tenure." "Hmm, tough!" said Dave continuing "You know, if you hire the Dean's daughter, everyone will assume you did it for tenure. On the other hand, if you hire Dante, people are going to wonder if you were *too close* to this whole thing. You know race is going to come up, to be frank with you, people are asking questions about this because you and Dante are both Black." With this Tyrell thanked Dave for his input and moved forward with a final review.

Now, having considered all the information and being aware of the potential impact on his career, the decision was at hand, and he was faced with a difficult choice. The committee was split with Tyrell's vote breaking the tie. It was clear that the committee respected Tyrell's decision, but there was an ulterior motive. Without a unanimous vote, the committee could point to Tyrell as the person responsible for choosing the new faculty member. This freed the committee members of any repercussions from the Dean or responsibility to the new diversity initiative.

Tyrell wasn't new to difficult decisions. During tighter times, WSCC had to make crucial cuts in order to maintain the financial viability of the college. Tyrell led the committee responsible for overseeing this process. This was new, however, as his decision would be scrutinized by the Dean and by other faculty members. The culture of WSCC had often paid lip service to diversity in the past, with little support for living up to the "hype." Also, while there is a nepotism policy in the Human Resources handbook, it has historically been ignored with family hires often made throughout the college. With the Search Committee divided, Tyrell was asked to make the final decision by the next morning.

STATEMENT OF PROBLEM

Take on the role of Tyrell. You have been charged with making the final recommendation of a new faculty member for the Biology Department at WSCC. Thoughtfully consider the factors involved and respond to the following questions.

- What are the key issues you are facing when considering hiring each candidate?
- What are your options and what are the pro's and con's of each option?
- Describe the culture at WSCC, and how culture may impact the decision you would make?
- What role does race and nepotism play in this case study? Consider Tyrell's decision in regards to Dante, the culture of WSCC, and the stance on diversity during the accreditation period at WSCC.
- What is the role of the Search Committee? With the information provided, how would you respond to the committee's willingness to pass the decision making power to you?
- Write a formal recommendation to the Dean and support your recommendation in a sound manner. Consider the implications of your decision when generating a response.
- Now consider that you have made your recommendation and have been approached by Dave. If asked what led to your decision, how would you respond? How would that response differ from that given to the Dean?

CASE STUDY 3

PAYING THE PRICE FOR TITLE IX SPORTS

David Horton Jr.

BACKGROUND

Westland Community College is a public two-year institution located in Winfield, Texas, a small rural west Texas town. According to the most recent census data, Westland has a total population of 3,557. WCC offers low-cost, state-supported educational programs to individuals from within its service district, across the state of Texas, and a small number of out-of-state and international students. The mission of WCC is to provide students with high-quality learning opportunities that promote personal and professional success in an ever-changing global environment. WCC is particularly focused on encouraging life-long learning and enhancing the quality of life of individuals in the communities they serve, by maintaining an open-door admissions policy and providing a comprehensive array of learning, service, and life experiences that will motivate and challenge their students to complete a degree or professional certificate.

Westland Community College has a student body population of 2,500 (60% female and 40% male). Most students that attend WCC commute to campus, are adult learners, and only attend part-time. Though viewed as a commuter campus, WCC does maintain five residence halls on campus with space to comfortably

Ethical Leadership and the Community College: Paradigms, Decision-Making, and Praxis, pages 133–136.

133

house 400 students. Over the past three years, the residence halls have been at full capacity as most of the available spaces in the halls are reserved for student-athletes, and those students that work directly with the athletics department. At WCC, student-athletes are a very noticeable group on campus—they comprise approximately 15% of the total student body[1]. Most student-athletes at WCC receive full or partial athletically-related financial aid, which can be used to cover their tuition and fees, books, meals and off campus housing. Over the past three years, nearly 80% of the student-athletes that have attended WCC have come from areas outside of WCC's service district or the state of Texas. At least 15% of student-athletes are international students. Westland is one of two higher education institutions located in Harris County—the other institution is a public four-year institution located in Wellington, which is approximately 50 miles west of Winfield. The next closest two-year institution is 145 miles west of Winfield. Westland is the only community college in west Texas that sponsors varsity athletics.

Westland has maintained a long history of support for athletics and student athletes. The current and past president of WCC both believe that athletics are an important part of the student experience, a valuable tool for recruiting athletes and non-athletes and a vehicle for connecting the campus to the local community. Westland is a Division I member of the National Junior College Athletic Association (NJCAA). The institution currently sponsors eight varsity team sports—Men's baseball, basketball, football, soccer and wrestling; and Women's basketball, softball, and volleyball. WCC's athletic operating budget during the 2010–2011 academic year was $1.5 million and total revenues generated during the same time period equaled $1.4 million. The ratio of operating expenses to revenues generated has stayed consistent over the past six years. As a result, the institution has been forced to subsidize a small portion of the athletics' budget each year.

STATEMENT OF THE PROBLEM

Over the past five years, WCC, like many community colleges throughout the U.S. has seen a drop in state financial support and revenues. As a result, between the 2009–2010 and 2010–2011 academic years, the institution was forced to release five full-time staff members and they also decided not to renew the contracts of two full-time faculty members in order to balance their operating budget. Currently, there are 30 full-time faculty and 100 full-time administrators and support staff employed at the institution. Not long after the college released these faculty and staff members, a local businessman and alumnus, Mr. Daniels, donated $2.5 million to the institution specifically to rebuild their Men's and Women's rodeo teams (after a five year hiatus), and to construct a new in-door arena for team practices and competitions.

---

[1] Note: This case is reflective of an actual institution that had a correspondingly high percentage of student athletes.

Though this gift is the largest single donation ever made to the institution in its 60 year history, the president has expressed to you some concerns about the institution accepting this gift and the financial implications of adding two more sports teams and up to 25 more student-athletes. Mr. Daniels' gift will cover the entire cost of constructing the new arena, but it will only cover the rodeo team's coaches salaries and student-athletes' scholarships for two years. After that time, the institution will be forced to subsidize the difference. Currently, the average head coaches' salary at WCC is $46,000, and the average assistant coaches' salary is $40,000. During the 2010–2011 academic year, athletically-related financial aid distributed to student-athletes exceeded $400,000. Because of recent budget constraints, there are little to no funds available for the added operational expenses that come with adding additional athletic teams and athletic coaches and staff. While the institution could initiative a fundraising campaign or seek out donations to fund the team, given the cuts being made to academic programs and faculty lines, the institution would rather focus its energies toward raising revenue for other areas (e.g., saving faculty jobs, and renovating older facilities).

On the other hand, there are many positives to accepting Mr. Daniel's gift. To start, these funds can be used to encourage other alumni and community members to contribute to the institution's fundraising campaign. Additionally, the new indoor arena could be used for events sponsored by the institution, the city of Westland and local high schools, which could ultimately bring additional revenues to the institution.

You have recently been promoted to Vice President for Student Services at Westland Community College. In this position you are responsible for overseeing all campus support programs, athletics, student activities, housing and food services. In your role as VP for Student Services, the College President, Dr. Perry, has asked you to put together a document detailing the implications of accepting or not accepting Mr. Daniels' gift. You have been given three weeks to complete this task. To complete this task, you must consider:

- What are the immediate political implications of accepting Mr. Daniels gift? What would be the implications of not accepting the gift? What are the long-term implications?
- How will support programs and campus services be impacted by the addition of two new athletics teams and additional student-athletes?
- What responsibility does the college have in terms of protecting financial resources for essential services versus using resources to grow and support its athletics program?
- What are the most effective solutions to meeting this unique situation, while limiting the long-term commitment of the institution to support these additional athletic teams and student-athletes?

- Are there any Title IX concerns that should be considered if two additional teams are added? If so, what are these concerns and what can be done to limit any possible Title IX violations?

CASE STUDY 4

VOLUNTEERS FOR SERVICE LEARNING

S. Mei-Yen Ireland and Ben Williams

BACKGROUND

Central Community College (CCC) is a two-year college located in a large Mid-Western city. CCC is the only community college in the metropolitan area, and serves over 25,000 full- and part-time students through its Career & Technical, Arts & Sciences, and Community Education & Workforce Development programs. The mission of the institution is: "To provide quality educational programs through a commitment to a robust curriculum for diverse learners. CCC strives to be responsive to the changing needs of our local community and the shifting technological demands of the global economy."

CCC is particularly well known and respected by the local community. Civic and business leaders, area educators, and community members appreciate the partnership offered by CCC to local businesses and organizations, and the success that its students and graduates have had through their post-secondary preparation. The college also has a higher rate of certificate and degree completion than similar urban community colleges in the state.

Ethical Leadership and the Community College: Paradigms, Decision-Making, and Praxis, pages 137–141.

For over 20 years, CCC has had a robust service-learning program, which has a strong reputation in the community because the program serves both the needs of the community and the needs of CCC students. The academic and co-curricular service-learning programs, run through the Office of Service-Learning and Community Partnerships, work with faculty, students, and community agencies to build reciprocal service-learning partnerships that positively impact student learning and community-identified outcomes. Successful programs include the after-school tutoring program, run in conjunction with the Early Childhood Education department, and an on-going service-learning course series through the Social Sciences Department, which partners students with local non-profit organizations, such as the food pantry, medical clinic, community garden program, and HIV/AIDS outreach center. In a recent Accreditation visit, the Social Sciences department's focus on service learning in their Sociology, Anthropology, and Cultural Diversity (multi-disciplinary) courses were noted as an exemplary "Best Practice" to facilitate critical thinking, civic engagement, and ethical decision making. In addition, feedback from community leaders has been very positive, in that the service-learning projects have helped to increase adult literacy. Additionally, teachers from the local schools have expressed appreciation for the extra tutoring students provide, and other organizations have shared that their services are higher quality and better able to manage increases in demand due to the important volunteer work of the CCC students. At the same time, some internal critics have noted that the service-learning component detracts from the core academic requirements of the course sequences, and there is also concern about the added time commitment required for students to fulfill their service-learning obligations.

CCC has increasingly felt pressure from state legislators and the Board of Regents to focus more on student success as measured by degree completion and transfer outcomes. The state is moving within the next biennium towards tying a larger portion of its funding of higher education to accountability measures that include degree completion and transfer rates. The President, Dr. Ethel Hamilton, has said in recent speeches to the campus and local community that she believes the best way to accomplish this goal is to reallocate funds across campus to strengthen student success over the course of the next two academic years, and beyond. In particular, President Hamilton has mentioned that she would like to strengthen the support provided to students (e.g., tutoring, mentoring, early warning policies) in order to increase transfer rates. President Hamilton believes funding should shift away from some of the service-learning programs to more "on-campus, student-centered, and academically rigorous" programs. This would address concerns about the added resources required to run successfully and manage multiple service-learning courses, and it would address internal criticisms about the lack of rigor within those courses and course sequences. She believes this will have a positive impact on the local community, though less direct, because more students will complete their degree objectives and transfer to four-year institutions. Within only a few miles of CCC are several small- to medium-sized four-year institutions, along with a large land-grant university with an enrollment of over 20,000 undergraduate students. President Hamilton's office has already received an out-pouring of concern from community agency staff and community leaders that this change in tone about community engagement will result in an elimination of the service-learning programs that are so valued by the local community.

KEY STAKEHOLDERS

- Dr. Justin(e) Griffith, *Director of Service-Learning and Community Part-nerships*: During your seven years as Director, the department of Service-Learning and Community Partnerships has expanded CCC's 20-year tradi-tion of robust service-learning programs, which has resulted in key student learning outcomes, such as critical thinking, civic engagement, and ethical decision making, and which has addressed community-identified needs. Dr. Griffith has built strong relationships with his/her supervisor, commu-nity agency staff and leaders, and service-learning faculty and students.
- Dr. Ethel Hamilton, *President*: Dr. Hamilton has served as president for two years. She was brought in by the board to expand the already successful CCC mission, and to increase revenue. Dr. Hamilton was formerly an aca-demic dean, and prior to that, an Economics professor.
- Dr. Erica Lane, *Vice President*: In her six years as the Vice President of CCC, Dr. Lane has been an avid supporter of the work of the Office of Ser-vice-Learning and Community Partnerships. She also wants to strengthen her relationship with the relatively new President, Dr. Hamilton.
- Stephanie Taylor and Marcus Johnson, *Community Agency Staff*: Ms. Tay-lor and Mr. Johnson work at two of the community agencies that host stu-dents in the service-learning courses. They have been active partners with CCC for nearly five years. They are particularly invested in maintaining the partnership with CCC, and believe that the role of the community col-lege is to serve the needs of the local community. They have found that the service-learning projects through CCC have encouraged a significant number of community members to pursue certificates and degrees at the college. They have seen the positive impact on those families affected.
- Mandy Williams, *Afterschool Program Coordinator*: Ms. Williams has coor-dinated the afterschool program for three years, and has recently begun an assessment project to research the impact of the program on the youth and CCC students who participate.
- Dr. David Howard, *Service-Learning Faculty:* Dr. Howard, who teaches So-ciology, is one of the faculty members who actively uses the Office of Service-Learning and Community Partnerships to develop his service-learning curriculum, and to connect students with local community agen-cies. He has worked at CCC for nearly ten years and feels passionately about the pedagogical uses of service-learning.

STATEMENT OF THE PROBLEM

President Hamilton has asked Dr. Lane to begin a process of restructuring the Office of Service-Learning and Community Partnership in order to direct more resources toward transfer programs, and to compel the service-learning faculty to "develop more academically rigorous curriculum." Dr. Lane is aware of the importance of maintaining and sustaining community relationships through this transition. Dr. Lane has asked you, as Director of Service-Learning and Community Partners, to implement an "into the streets" annual campus-wide service day in which students will volunteer in the community with various community agencies to restore good-will and trust between the community and CCC. She wants you to reduce the number of ongoing, semester-long service-learning programs in favor of more one-time projects that work with a variety of agencies and cost less money and less staff time to implement.

Stephanie Taylor, Marcus Johnson, and Mandy Williams have left you several distraught voicemails because they are concerned about the long-term implications of no longer having a steady, reliable pool of volunteers for their programs. They are particularly upset that they are being asked to find new projects to accommodate hundreds of students for a one-day project. They cite the fact that they have lots of needs for on-going volunteers at two of the local elementary schools, the local Food Pantry, and a community Literacy Programs. They have few, if any, needs for one-time volunteers. Additionally, their programs working with kids and marginalized populations require relationship-building, therefore they are not comfortable having one-time volunteer students work with their clients. The local industry leaders are also aware, but have expressed concern, about the shift away from service-learning, despite recognizing the potential positive outcomes from increasing transfer and completion rates. It is important to note that city officials recently raised concerns in a News Conference about the lack of services for the poorest members of the community at a time when those community resources are being cut due to a recent recession.

Professor Howard has approached you on behalf of the service-learning faculty members who are concerned that your office will no longer help them establish the community partnerships for their service-learning classes. The faculty members believe this will significantly alter their curriculum, and they feel that President Hamilton's comments about what constitutes "rigorous curriculum" are insulting, and infringe on their academic freedom. Professor Howard demands a meeting with you and Vice President Lane.

Given your role at CCC as the primary bridge between the community and college, your leadership is needed to address the President's shift in focus while navigating your relationships with your supervisor, faculty, community agency staff and community leaders.

QUESTIONS TO CONSIDER:

- Where should you start? What are your priorities?
- What are the values of service-learning? What role does community voice and input play in decision-making? What might be problematic about an annual campus-wide service day?
- What are the responsibilities of the community college to the community? How does service-learning fit (or not fit) with these responsibilities?
- What are some effective ways to communicate with the stakeholders involved in this case?
- What are the long-term implications of the President's shift in focus?
- What are the various power dynamics at play in this situation?
- Given the president's commitment toward the reallocation of resources to promote student success and transfer outcomes, are there any alternative solutions? What are the advantages and disadvantages of these alternatives?
- Community respect and trust are threatened by the proposed changes in the service-learning work at CCC. What strategies can be used to address this sentiment?
- How might you use best practices, research, and learning outcomes from the faculty's service-learning course to make a case for the value of service-learning?
- What other issues need to be considered as you decide how to address this complex situation which has multiple implications for internal and external stakeholders?

CASE STUDY 5

FACILITATING STUDENT SUCCESS AND LONG-TERM FISCAL STABILITY

Jim Riggs

BACKGROUND

Arizona Community College (ACC) is located in a region that is experiencing a major shift in population with a growing number of retirees and a decline in traditional college age students and families. The shift is mostly due to a change in the region's economic base, from natural resources and agriculture to service industries and tourism. The region is a desirable place to live with affordable housing and numerous services for retirees, but there are few jobs with livable wages available. The college experienced steady enrollment growth of over four percent each year for the past ten years. However, with the region's shifting demographics, including a rapid rise in the median age and educational level of the population, coupled with the sharp decline in the number of students attending and graduating from the local K–12 public schools, it was clear the college's enrollment growth will not continue. ACC along with other community colleges throughout the country have relied upon modest growth in enrollment each year in order to maintain fiscal stability and expand programs and services.

Ethical Leadership and the Community College: Paradigms, Decision-Making, and Praxis,
pages 143–147.
Copyright © 2014 by Information Age Publishing
All rights of reproduction in any form reserved.

Most of the faculty and staff have worked at ACC for several years and were hired specifically to develop the instructional and student services programs. This has created strong ownership and a sense of pride in these programs. With the exception of adding new programs and services, there has been little change in the college's operations and organization for the past 20 years.

Near the end of the weekly cabinet meeting with the college's three vice presidents, the college president, Dr. Bernard, moved from the usual agenda items that focused on the immediate business of the college to what he referred to as something much more urgent, the future of the college. Dr. Bernard indicated that he had reviewed data from several sources and "it appears that we have a perfect storm developing at the college." The president then handed out a fact sheet that clearly showed that local public schools had been losing enrollment for the past four years at a rate of 10 percent per year, and the projected number of high school graduates was expected to decrease by nearly 25 percent within the next five years. The fact sheet also highlighted that much of the growth the college had experienced over the past decade actually came from an increase in part-time students who were taking courses for personal enrichment, which were mostly retirees. This surprised the vice presidents. They believed the college had done a good job expanding its offerings and reaching out to new pools of students. The vice presidents, like many at the college, assumed the mainstay of its growth enrollment had been in full-time traditional aged students, who were pursuing either transfer degrees or vocational degrees and certificates.

The president made it clear ACC must refocus its efforts on retaining its existing students instead of relying on enrollment growth. Dr. Bernard also raised another disturbing problem that was masked by years of enrollment growth, only one third of the full-time students who begin one of the college's occupational degree programs or university transfer programs ever finished. He declared that the college needs to find better ways to assist and facilitate students toward degree completion. After a great deal of discussion between the president and vice presidents, Dr. Bernard asserted, "we need to figure out how to transform the college and reposition all our instructional, learning support, and student development programs to do a better job retaining the students."

Dr. Bernard was convinced that the college's traditional organizational structure, with separate and distinct divisions for student services, instruction, and administrative services was working against developing any real solutions and allowing too many students to fail. He believed that increasing cooperation and collaboration between programs and services would do little to fix the underlying organizational problems. President Bernard was certain the only way to address these problems was to consolidate these separate and isolated programs and services into an integrated and cohesive network, and this would require a complete reorganization. He told the vice presidents, "we have evolved into a bureaucratic and self-serving institution where everyone has carved out their little territories and built their own silos." The president pointed out there were nine different tutoring and learning lab programs spread throughout the campus with four housed under the instructional division and five under the student services division. He noted that the college had more than a dozen different student support programs that operate virtually independently of each other. The president also pointed out that at the beginning of each semester students were required to go to at least four different locations scattered around the college in order to register, pay their fees, and pick up their financial aid checks. He then asserted that there was "no reason why these basic transactions couldn't happen in one location and be done by the same person. We have set up a bewildering maze for students." The president went on, "while we say we are about student success, what it looks like to me is that we are really about maintaining a comfortable work environment and the status quo, and have forgotten about our students. We need to turn the process upside down and look at it from the students' point of view."

The president noted the college was now in a much different economic climate. "The data speak for themselves. If we continue to operate like we have been, we are likely to experience a rapid decline in enrollment that will cause a downward spiral in funding and fewer opportunities for students. We cannot keep living on our past successes."

STATEMENT OF THE PROBLEM

You are one of the vice presidents and agreed that there were some problems with the current organizational structure, but by and large, you and the other vice presidents believed the employees in all three divisions were truly concerned about student success. Collectively, you worried that any sort of suggestion to change the way the college was organized would be met with strong resistance by faculty and staff. The vice president of instruction, Dr. Bass, visibly upset by the idea of reorganization, stated the college had a long tradition of respecting the autonomy of the faculty members and instructional programs.

Dr. MacGregor, vice president of student services, then argued it was the employees who knew best what students needed, and that "the administration should be careful about getting in the staff's way of working with students." The vice presidents then suggested several ways in which they could create greater cooperation among some of the programs in their divisions. However, Dr. Bernard reiterated his stance that what was needed was a full, college-wide integration and consolidation of programs and services to improve retention and student success in order to keep the college financially sound. The president indicated the only way he envisioned the college could get there was by reorganizing from three divisions into two divisions. One division would house all instructional, student development, and learning support programs. This would allow for all programs and services that focus on student learning and success to be housed in the same division. The other division would include business services, health and safety, student financial systems including financial aid, student enrollment services, all technology services, facilities, and human resources. He indicated the two new divisions would be led by a vice president and be supported by a network of deans and directors.

Dr. Bernard then stated that while he believed his plan would be the best way to move the college forward, he would be open to other ideas that could dramatically improve student retention and success. This, however, was followed by a directive to the vice presidents to develop a reorganization plan that would advance student learning, be cost neutral, and to the extent possible, have employee buy-in. The plan would serve as a guide for building a new college-wide structure that would "facilitate and advance student learning as the center/core of all college functions and actions." The president made it clear, "if the plan works well, the college should see a dramatic increase in student retention and success, and at the same time, break our dependency on annual enrollment growth." He ended the meeting by stating the college would need to undergo nothing short of major transformation, shifting from being employee focused to one future oriented and focused on student learning and success.

You and the other vice presidents know that any plan that required substantial change would likely be met with stiff resistance throughout the college community. You asked the president to give you time to work with your divisions. The president reluctantly agreed and indicated that he expected each division to report back their efforts and results within the next two months. The vice presidents agreed that for any reorganization plan to work, you would need the support of everyone at the college. The vice presidents also realized that if the president's reorganization plan was put into place, one of you would likely lose your position.

The next day you, Dr. MacGregor, and Dr. Bass meet to discuss what could be done to improve student retention and degree completion, and to start a conversation about developing a reorganization plan. All three of you are quite concerned about how to approach faculty and staff to get buy-in, knowing that without widespread support for a new organizational structure, there would be little or no progress in improving student retention and success rates. As a first step, you decide to host an all college meeting to review the data on the changing demographics of the region and the disconcerting high school graduation projections with the idea of starting an institution wide conversation on how the college might stay financially strong over the next several years without enrollment growth. You decide to wait and see where the conversation goes in the meeting before bringing up the idea of reorganization.

Later that week an announcement went out inviting all the employees to a "strategic conversation" entitled, *Strengthening Student Retention and Student Success—A College-Wide Mandate*. The announcement said nothing about enrollment problems or any pending college-wide reorganization plans. Dr. Bernard immediately responds to the vice presidents by sending a confidential e-mail to the vice presidents reminding them to address the issues associated with the underlying organizational problems, and that he expects a reorganization plan within the next few months. He encourages the vice presidents to be straight with the college community about the enrollment challenges and fiscal realities facing the college over the next several years. He tells you not to shy away from having an open and honest discussion about the organizational challenges, and that the college will need to be reorganized to better support students. He ended the e-mail by stating, "We have excellent programs and services, that is not the problem. The problem that needs to be solved is how to reorganize and integrate these programs and services into a cohesive network that will lead to greater student retention and success."

Right before the all college meeting, you along with Dr. Bass and Dr. Mac-Gregor have a quick conversation about the e-mail and decide that while you agree with the president that a reorganization of the college is needed, you would stick to your original plan to see where the conversation goes before saying anything about a reorganization plan, agreeing that you do not want to "derail" any creative brainstorming. You recognize that, as the senior leaders of the college, it is up to you to shepherd the long overdue transformation. You also recognize that part of the challenge is to manage the expectations of the college president who is insisting on significantly changing the college organization structure. You know if the college is going to be successful in dramatically improving student retention and completion rates and move away from dependency on incremental growth funding, it would require a herculean effort on the part of all faculty, staff, and college administrators. All three of you recognize that the hardest part was now ahead of them. The "perfect storm" mentioned by the president was likely to be much bigger than he projected. As you and the other vice presidents work to carry out the president's directive, consider the following:

- A strong identity among the employees is tied to these traditional divisions. What are some of the strategies that could be used to reduce this sense of loss and resentment in order to get employees to support the organizational changes?
- What are some effective ways that could be used to minimize confusion and disruption to the ongoing operations of the college when implementing these administrative and organizational changes?
- How might the vice president use the research on best practices in the areas of student engagement, retention and instructional innovations to help convince the faculty to support the organizational changes?
- What should the vice presidents be doing ahead of time to anticipate and address the numerous human resources matters including bargaining unit concerns and employee classification issues?
- Given how strongly the president feels about how the college should be reorganized, should the vice presidents' propose an alternative plan? If so, what would it look like and how might they persuade the president to move forward with their plan?

CASE STUDY 6

TO RESTRICT OR NOT

Tuition and Fee Waivers for Immigrant Students

Juanita Gamez Vargas

Rural Community College (RCC) has experienced many changes in the last 20 years. The college is located in the center of town, population 35,000 and enrolls 2100 full and part-time students. The average student is 25 years old, the gender make-up is 60% women and 40% male and ethnic diversity is 85% White, 12 % Latino, 1.5 % African-American, and 1.5% Cambodian. RCC serves as a feeder college to Rural State University (RSU). Over 95% of the students receive some form of financial aid.

Joaquin Johnson moved up from the faculty ranks to president of RCC. Vaughn Meiller is VP for Instruction, Becky Gates is VP for Student Services, and Attila T. Hun is VP for Business Services. RCC receives their funding from state and local tax funds. RCC, just like other community colleges across the country, has experienced drastic cuts in federal, state and local funding. RCC has kept tuition rate increases to less than 5% annually. Although students have complained about the tuition increases, enrollment continues to climb.

Johnson hired a new foundation director three years ago, Amy Smart, who recently started an alumni program. Smart diversified her foundation board to include more RCC alumni and business owners. One successful RCC founda-

Ethical Leadership and the Community College: Paradigms, Decision-Making, and Praxis,
pages 149–151.

tion program, Rural Achievement (RA), provides free tuition and fees for county area high school graduates who score in the top ten percent in their class. Rural Achievement is credited for low-income and first-generation students accessing college. Over 50% of the RA graduates transfer to RSU and 50% of those students earn their bachelor degrees within four years.

The 2010 census reports that the demographics have drastically shifted in regards to race and ethnicity. The Latino population has increased from 1.2% (2000 census) to 15.97 %. In the last ten years, the business community lost a number of manufacturing companies and increased in the number of poultry and pig production and packaging. Most of the Latino immigrants work in the new companies. Mary Martinez, a RCC graduate, owns one of the poultry companies and offers her employees financial incentives for attending RCC. Another RCC graduate, Guadalupe Lopez, owns three small retail businesses and chairs the local Chamber of Commerce. Martinez and Lopez are two of fifteen Mexican undocumented immigrants who graduated from RCC because of the tuition-free incentive. Of the remaining 13 students, five transferred and graduated from RSU. Currently, over 30 siblings and extended relatives of the original 15 attend RCC in addition to Martinez' employee educational incentive program.

STATEMENT OF THE PROBLEM

During a recent budget meeting, RCC Board member Rudy Hoess suggested eliminating the RA program as a cost cutting measure. Hoess rationalized that the top ten percent high school graduates receive scholarships at universities eliminating the need for a RA program at a community college. Lewis Dolls brought up the issue of the free tuition and fee incentive for undocumented immigrants. Dolls states that the Mexican immigrants are too high in number and the college should restrict the tuition and fee waivers to American-born students only. Another board member states that all Mexican high school graduates are "anchor babies," and therefore, should not receive the tuition and fee waivers. The conversation escalates to comments about "illegal aliens" receiving a free American education, social justice and drug cartels taking over the country. RCC President Johnson and Board President William Clinton try to bring order to the meeting. Johnson states that he will provide a report to the board at the next meeting on the RA program as a potential cost-cutting measure. The Board agrees. After the meeting, Johnson and Clinton discuss their surprise over some comments made by the Board members about the RA program and immigrants. Clinton (who is married to Mary Martinez) expresses support for the RA program and wants a pre-Board meeting briefing on Johnson's report. Johnson agrees.

Johnson meets the next day with key members of his organization. In attendance are Meiller, Gates, Hun and Smart. As the community college president, Johnson wants to respond to the Board's request on the RA program from a variety of decision-making perspectives: bureaucratic, ethical, and policy. Johnson asks for input for strategizing his response. Johnson's goal is for RCC continue to offer the RA incentive regardless of the student's immigration status. Johnson asks Hun to identify other areas for potential cuts, if necessary. Huns nods in agreement. Smart states she will gather historical data on the RA program, i.e., number of students receiving tuition and fees, funding sources, success stories from inception to now. However, Smart does not have the data on degree completion or transfers to the university. Gates interjects and volunteers to obtain data on RA transfers and degree completions. Gates also states she can check on the RA student's legal status, but needs to maintain confidentiality. Hun will review the college's charter and policy handbook on services for undocumented students for compliance verification. At this point, everyone turns to Johnson and asks if they are on target in achieving his goal? Will these strategies address the goals set out by Johnson?

As Meiller, you have remained quiet wondering whether you agree with Johnson's strategy on the RA program to all qualifying students, regardless of their immigration status. You philosophically agree with RCC's mission of "providing access to excellent workforce and transfer programs, student services, and continuing education that promotes student success...." However, the comments made by the Board on undocumented students did not surprise you. With the exception of Clinton and three other board members, the remaining five Board members are known for their racially bias views.

QUESTIONS

- What are the consequences of experiencing a change in racial/ethnic campus demographics?
- What are the implications of keeping or eliminating the RA program?
- What other strategic goals would you suggest to Johnson and the team in supporting the RA program to all qualifying students regardless of their immigration status?
- What, if any, is the responsibility of the board, campus administrators, and faculty members in facilitating the success of immigrant students?

CASE STUDY 7

NOT SO SUNNY IN SUNNY TOWN COMMUNITY COLLEGE

Samer Batarseh and Rafael Prado

BACKGROUND

Sunny Community College (SCC) is a California community college located in a rapidly growing town surrounded by farms and canaries. The town has a diverse population of 75,000 people. SCC's ethnic composition is the following: 45 percent Latino, 12 percent Asians, 8 percent Black, and 35 percent Caucasian. SCC is the only postsecondary institution within a 100-mile radius of Sunny Town. SCC is operating under California's open access policy and only requires mathematics and English placement exams for admittance. High school graduation rates in Sunny Town based on ethnic background are as follows: 52 percent Latino, 94 percent Asian, 61 percent Black, and 89 percent White. Forty-seven percent of the student body at SCC is enrolled in remedial courses such as Basic Reading, Writing or Pre-Algebra.

STATEMENT OF THE PROBLEM

As a result of hard economic conditions, SCC has been experiencing a decrease in state funding. The achievement gap among high school students from different

Ethical Leadership and the Community College: Paradigms, Decision-Making, and Praxis,
pages 153–155.
Copyright © 2014 by Information Age Publishing

ethnic backgrounds is an evident challenge. Moreover, the achievement gap and success rates for the different ethnic groups is duplicated at the college level. SCC has suffered from high dropout rates in remedial courses.

The new president of the college, Dr. Sharp, who had previously been a corporate executive, was able to show the local business community the 'win/win' approach of increasing the number of college graduates from SCC. Through financial modeling and effective communication methods, President Sharp managed to secure donations from private businesses to help SCC. Dr. Sharp would like to utilize the donated funds to transform SCC to a 21st college by modernizing the main computer lab and offer more computer classes (along with building a new student union, gymnasium, and building a high-tech facility with SMART rooms). Dr. Sharp believes that offering more computer courses will attract more students who believe that a college degree is something that can help them land a better job at a local business or assist them in transferring to a four-year college (resulting in a lower dropout rate). Dr. Sharp asserts that the use of new computer technologies to teach remedial courses would help the college meet the current demand for remediation in mathematics, reading, and writing. Also, the computer lab can easily serve students who are taking college level courses in computer science, math, science, and visual arts.

Dr. Sharp's vision is facing resistance from the faculty senate and teachers' union. The faculty senate at SCC would like to hire more staff to meet the demand for remedial courses, which they believe would increase enrollment and lower dropout rates. The faculty senate believes that the current faculty members have been overworked and need extra assistance immediately. Morale among faculty has been low, especially since the implementation of a no raise policy and a hiring freeze two years ago. The faculty senate believes that expanding the workload for current faculty should be a short-term fix, and the root cause of the problem (hiring new full- time faculty) should be remedied as soon as possible. The teachers' union would like the president to use the new funds to provide temporary pay raises to current members who have not received any raises for the past few years. The teachers' union believes that SCC faculty members are getting paid less than their peers in other community colleges in California.

In the next two years, SCC will also need to revisit its contractual obligations with the faculty union. This process could be very contentious due to the tight economic constraints of the college, the insistence of the union leadership for a salary increase and cost of living allowance. The union is unwilling to compromise on the latter due to its prior agreements of a hiring freeze, and an increase of its members' monthly contributions towards health insurance costs and retirement benefits.

Moreover, SCC is having to address areas of improvement mandated by the accreditation audit. The college needs to make a number of improvements in the areas of teacher/student ratio, part-time/full-time faculty ratios, technology access issues for students, modifications to facilities for students with disabilities under the Americans with Disabilities Act, student learning outcomes, and earthquake retrofitting to its antiquated facilities. Also, SCC's nationally recognized athletic program is in jeopardy due to budget cuts. This could include reduction in pre-season games, away games, and number of individual and team sport offerings. The college must continue to comply with Title IX which requires an equitable appropriation of funding between men and women programs.

Overall, there is a sense of mistrust between faculty members and administration at SCC. The new president is an external hire, and is not yet aware of the intricate details of power struggles and politics within the college. The faculty feels that they are under appreciated by administration as evident with the absence of raises and the hiring freeze policies. Finally, SCC is finding it difficult to comply with the Clery Act when it comes to reporting crimes on campus in a timely fashion. This includes hiring additional safety officers and replacing its fired campus chief of police due to his ineptitude to enforce the Clery Act mandates on campus. These safety problems need to be addressed immediately if the college wants to continue to offer federal financial aid. The issue of proper use of funding is complicated in nature and poignant to some stakeholders. If you were the new president of SCC, how would you respond to the current situation and the following issues?

- How would you, as a new president, prioritize the challenges facing the college? Which ones are more eminent and need to be addressed immediately? Why?
- How would you empower your staff and faculty to create a more collaborative culture at SCC and establish common goals?
- How would you improve morale among faculty members without increasing their salaries?
- How would you respond to the demands by the faculty senate to use the funds to hire more faculty members?
- How would you respond to the demands by the teachers' union to use the funds to pay for raises for current faculty?

CASE STUDY 8

BETWEEN A ROCK
AND A HARD PLACE

Addressing the Divide

Walter A. Torrence, III

BACKGROUND

Pacific Community College (PCC) is a mixed residential and commuter two-year community college located in the far northern region of California. It is the lone community college in a two county area with a population of approximately 220,000. The college's population consists of 15,500 students. Of these students, 52% attend part-time while 48% are full-time attendees; 79% of students are Whites, with most students 84% being from both first-generation and low-income backgrounds. The average age of the student population is 24.8, with 36% of students ranging from 18–24 years of age, and 37% from 25 to 31 years of age. The remaining 27% of the population range from 32 to 68 years of age. The most popular majors on campus are in the behavioral and social sciences (e.g., sociology, psychology, political science).

Recently, the Vice President of Academic Affairs, Dr. Stillwater, has uncovered a disturbing trend. While there has been a steady increase of students declar-

Ethical Leadership and the Community College: Paradigms, Decision-Making, and Praxis, pages 157–161.

ing one or more of the behavioral and social sciences as majors; there has been a sharp decline in the percentage of students majoring in Science, Technology, Engineering, and Mathematics (STEM) fields. In fact, in the last ten years, the percentage of STEM majors has fallen from 45% to 20%; a rate of 2.5% per year. Within a national context, colleges from around the nation have begun to focus on increasing the production of STEM majors to aid the nation in competing in a global market economy. In addition, in order to keep these departments afloat, there is a need to generate enrollment in these fields, as failing to do so may result in the elimination and merging of existing programs and faculty.

Dr. Stillwater has an aggressive goal for remedying this problem; she wishes to see the total proportion of STEM majors increase by ten percent within two academic school years. Dr. Stillwater is annoyed with the division of Student Affairs, particularly personnel in Recruitment and Admissions. She feels they have either ignored or is unaware of the downward trend of STEM majors. The board of trustees and President of the college have regularly talked about the importance of improving STEM student degree production. The negligence in this area creates an issue for two particular reasons. Firstly, the campus has less ability to apply for National Science Foundation (NSF) funding. Secondly, this puts a strain on relationships with four-year institutions seeking transfer students with backgrounds in STEM fields. As a result, Dr. Stillwater decides to put together a team of academic affairs administrators and faculty to develop a recruitment program specifically targeting students interested in STEM majors.

Based on past practice, Dr. Stillwater recognizes that recruitment is typically a function of student affairs. However, given the critical need to produce more STEM graduates, she believes it is important for academic affairs to take the lead in this area. She knows that doing so may result in tension between academic and student affairs; however, relations between these two groups are already strained (as a result of more than a decade of fighting between camps). As such, she believes it is unrealistic for a collaborative effort to be made in this regard. Thus, Dr. Stillwater moves forward with her efforts without giving a 'heads up' or including the Director of Recruitment and Admissions in the planning process. Only amongst loyal staff members does Stillwater refer to the program as a recruitment program; to all others, the program is billed as a mentoring program for incoming STEM majors. Dr. Stillwater mentions the desire to engage in the program in passing conversation with the President who thought it sounded like a good idea. Dr. Stillwater's planning team worked diligently from the start of the fall semester (in August) for over two months. They have created recruitment brochures, a unified message, identified target high schools (in and out of the region), and have even developed an interactive website to facilitate recruitment efforts. In all, while some glitches still need to be worked out, the planning team believes that the program is ready for launch.

In January, the program sends STEM faculty and students to high schools within a 100 mile radius of campus. The targeted students are provided detailed information about STEM majors. In classroom speeches, they provide students with information on major options, median earnings, and career pathways. At two college fairs, students are given the opportunity to test their STEM skills/abilities in a number of fun and challenging puzzles. The program earns praise from every school visited and the number of intended STEM majors start to rise. After only two weeks of operation, Stillwater deems the program to be an initial success. Moving quickly, Dr. Stillwater drafts a short memo to the President, outlining the operations of the program, initial successes, and asks the President for permission to submit a full report accompanied with a funding request to be considered for the following years' budgetary cycle.

As expected, it does not take long for news of the Dr. Stillwater's program proposal to reach Jeremy Dutton, Director of Recruitment and Admissions. In fact, Dutton had heard rumors that academic affairs was putting together a STEM program, but did not have details on the exact nature of the program. Dutton never expected that it would be an outreach program, assuming they were developing a mentoring or tutoring program. In fact, at some point, Dutton believes that someone mentioned a STEM mentoring program being created by academic affairs, but doesn't remember the specifics. Dutton has been on leave for undisclosed health reasons, having his Assistant Director serve as interim during the entire fall semester. Talk from the campus 'rumor-mill' indicated that Dutton had cancer and would not be returning for the Spring semester. To the surprise of many, he returned and looks pretty healthy.

Unfortunately, Dutton learns of the efforts only after his college outreach representatives phone him (with concern about the status of their jobs) from a college fair (his first week back on the job) where both groups are hosting separate booths. Dutton is outraged and immediately relays the information to the Vice President of Student Affairs, Dr. Lance. Dr. Stillwater learns from her staff that the 'cat is out of the bag,' but admittedly, was surprised that the efforts had went on for several months without student affairs even knowing about it (she sees this as even further evidence of their incompetence).

Enraged, Dr. Lance (VP of Student Affairs) takes the issue to the President. He informs the President that Dr. Stillwater has blatantly overstepped divisional boundaries and launched a program which should have (at the very least) been brought to the attention of or (more appropriately) spearheaded by the Recruitment and Admissions office. He also expresses his concern that the manner in which student affairs learned of the program is professionally reprehensible, noting that his outreach staff were terrified, as they believed that their positions were being replaced. He noted that he has also 'just learned' of Dr. Stillwater's proposal to expand the program and suggests that it should not be taken into consideration.

The President listens to Dr. Lance's statements and decides to arrange a meeting with both Dr. Stillwater and Dr. Lance, in hope that a resolution can be worked out. The meeting is quite heated, with both sides standing firm on their belief that they are in the right. It becomes obvious that a compromise or collaborative effort is beyond reach. As such, an executive decision must be made as how to decide the most effective way of moving forward. You inform Drs. Stillwater and Lance that you will make a decision about the program within the coming weeks.

STATEMENT OF THE PROBLEM

You are the President of PCC, and with the development of the STEM recruitment program, you are placed in a delicate position. On a personal level, you have been longtime friends with both Drs. Stillwater and Lance. This has required a delicate balance of personal and professional relationships on your part, especially given the tension between the two. In fact, fact, you have known both of them for over 30 years, sharing many mutual friends (on campus and off campus). This has made dealing with the tension between the two very difficult. Tradition, history, relationships, and local culture are important values in the region; frankly, firing or demoting one or both of them would be political suicide.

To be truthful, you feel the program is an amazing idea. The program fills a lot of benefits for the institution; it positions the campus for NSF funding, makes campus students highly sought out for transfer, and increases the prestige of the institution. Further, you cannot see your current cadre of student affairs staff developing a program with this level of success given the fractured state of their leadership. You have received word some of the visited high schools have spread the word about the program to other schools outside of the targeted 100 mile radius, and they are hoping the program will visit their schools as well. On the other hand, you understand quite well the position the student affairs division has been placed in, being that recruitment and admissions is a function that has historically resided under their jurisdiction. While you were aware that academic affairs were engaged in some recruitment efforts in STEM, you assumed (or hoped) that some degree of communication had already taken place between your leadership team. You don't exactly remember the full conversation that you had about the recruitment efforts prior to their launch, beyond telling Dr. Stillwater that it sounded like a good idea, 'run with it.' Most of your time is spent off-campus raising money to fund institutional operations and expansion, this issue is an unwanted nuisance.

In all, the issue has been distracting from more important issues (e.g., budget cuts, public scrutiny, accreditation reaffirmation). You need to be able to trust your leadership team; this constant infighting has to stop. On a personal level, your contract is coming up for renewal in a few months; several board members have already expressed concern about your inability to handle inter-organizational politics (particularly the academic and student affairs divide). However, you are worried that addressing this issue could cause a greater fracture in personnel relations. You perceive the board members as politicians who don't understand the intricate dynamics of day-to-day campus operations. As an alumnus of the institution, you want what is best for the campus, and understand your decision could have a lasting impact on how successful the college will be—going forward. You have to address this issue quickly. In making your decision, you must consider (at least) the following: a) the ongoing friction between academic and student affairs; b) that Dr. Stillwater is working on a project which is outside of his jurisdiction; c) the pilot run of the program showed an increase in students interested in STEM fields; d) more high schools are requesting that the program attend their respective college fairs; e) PCC's relationships with four-year institutions could be enhanced by filling their STEM student pipeline needs; and f) your review is coming up soon.

Consider the following questions:

- Should you fund STEM outreach program?
- Which house (academic or student affairs) should the program operate in?
- How do you resolve the chasm between academic and student affairs?
- How do you position your actions to ensure your own reappointment?

CASE STUDY 9

MERGING THE DIVIDE

Equitable Articulation Agreements

Dionica Bell

BACKGROUND

Lillian Reed is the Dean of Admissions and Records at Rock Creek Community College (RCCC). She has served in this capacity for the past seven years. She was previously the Assistant Director of Admissions at RCCC, but left for a Director post at Harbor View Community College. Lillian was missed while at Harbor View. She was well liked at Rock Creek. People saw her as charismatic and dedicated to her job. Students remarked how approachable she was and faculty found her personable. Ultimately, Lillian returned to RCCC, after a little coercion from her long time mentor at Rock Creek, to apply for the position of Dean. Fortunately, Lillian was successful in the hiring process and obtained the post.

Lillian's transition back to Rock Creek was easy. She missed the campus were she'd cut her administrative 'teeth.' Rock Creek is in an urban setting, and serves 4,030 students who tended to be non-traditional, low income, minority, and first generation students. This is exactly the type of student population that Lillian enjoys serving. She never felt quite at home during her stint at Harbor View, as they served a more affluent, homogenous student population. The students at Harbor

Ethical Leadership and the Community College: Paradigms, Decision-Making, and Praxis,
pages 163–169.
Copyright © 2014 by Information Age Publishing

View came from academically rigorous high schools and usually were enrolled to finish their general education and transfer to Red Valley University after being denied as freshman. In contrast to Harbor View, Rock Creek students often need remediation, but go on to become strong and prepared transfer students and graduates.

Since her return to Rock Creek, Lillian has been committed to improving the transfer rate from Rock Creek to Red Valley University. Red Valley, the flagship university in the tri-state area boasts high graduation rates, low faculty to student ratios and an impressive $500 million endowment. As result of their success, the institution is ranked in the top 20 by *U.S. News and World Report*. The students at RVU tend be affluent, traditionally aged (18 to 24) and White. While at Harbor view, she was a part of team that was able to negotiate an articulation agreement for guaranteed admissions into Red Valley. She's been unable to duplicate that at Rock Creek despite continued pressure from RCCC's President and the Board of Trustees. Through her previous collaborations, Lillian forged important relationships with administrators. She promised to leverage those relationships at Red Valley to her superiors at Rock Creek to improve relations and transfer rates. Red Valley has typically been apprehensive to take RCCC students, citing that they have low first semester persistence rates, substandard preparation (particularly with respect to writing ability). Lillian hasn't seen any evidence to support this claim and other four-year institutions have not had the same issues with RCCC transfers. Lillian believes there is stigma associated with RCCC students (due to the demographic characteristics of the students), and these issues are a result of perceptions from Red Valley faculty and administration. To further complicate matters, the few students who are accepted from Rock Creek are challenged by Red Valley's apprehension to accept RCCC coursework. In some cases, students can lose 20 to 30 credits upon transfer, an issue not experienced when transferring to other institutions in the region. Lillian's students at Harbor View didn't experience these same course transfer challenges, so she believes this circumstance could be purposeful, in order to discourage RCCC students from even attempting to attend Red Valley.

Lillian has made attempt after attempt to create 50 guaranteed admission spots for Rock Creek students to transfer to Red Valley each year, based upon meeting a set of criteria. The criteria are similar to other existing articulation agreements with several of the community colleges in the city. Red Valley keeps feigning interest to sign an agreement, but has yet to do so. Recently, Lillian has been afforded an opportunity that most administrators in her position can only dream of. She has a unique chance to form a partnership with Alexandra Nichols, a RCCC graduate and local business mogul. While at Harbor View, Lillian and Alexandra negotiated a large gift to the college and scholarships for students who transfer to Red Valley University. Alexandra attended Red Valley as a transfer student from RCCC and has excelled ever since.

Alexandra has discussed her plan with the President of Red Valley, who assured her of his institutions commitment to creating an articulation agreement with RCCC, for *all* RCCC students that meet the following criteria: Students must have a minimum grade point average of a 3.30; have taken all necessary general education pre-requisites; have attempted and completed those classes within of the past four years; and must have (at least some) research exposure. Lillian is elated to hear this news, but knows the criteria (which are more extensive than the criteria for Harbor Valley students) will be difficult to meet. That being said, this is just the type of initiative that Lillian needs to position herself for the Vice President of Student Services (VPSS) position, which is about to come available due to an impending retirement by the current VPSS. Given that she has served in her current position for seven years, she feels that the time is ripe to step up in rank and authority.

Lillian recognizes that in order for Rock Creek to achieve several of the tenants suggested for the articulation agreement, institutional changes must be made. The President of RCCC has tasked Lillian, with the help of the Vice President of Academic Affairs, Chad Bowman, to put together an Ad-hoc committee to help with facilitation. They will co-chair the committee. The group is tasked with creating a plan that can successfully pass substantial programmatic changes through the faculty senate (with a possible need to obtain faculty union approval). Chad assembled some of the most influential people at the college, as he noted that they were the only leaders capable of getting the changes made. Chad is a very democratic leader so it's important to him that everyone has a voice in the decision-making process. This approach often slows down change at RCCC. However, Chad has only been at Rock Creek for a year and a half. Chad tends to change institutions often in order to receive promotions. As a result of his transiency, he hasn't formed many strong relationships, as of yet. Some faculty members on campus don't trust him, but also don't expect him to be around for long.

The President of the Faculty Senate, Diana Lynch, is also on the committee. She has been at Rock Creek for 15 years. Diana is and has always been concerned with the quality of teaching taking place at Rock Creek. Neither Lillian nor Diana trust Chad's motives. Diana has an eye on Chad's position and isn't interested in seeing him succeed. She's ready for him to move on so she can begin the 'real work' of improving the quality of education at Rock Creek. Diana believes getting RCCC students into Red Valley is an opportunity for the institution to gain prestige. As such, she wants to support the establishment of programmatic structure which enhances transfer opportunities.

Marla Pearson, the fourth member of the committee, is the Faculty Union president and a fixture of the university. There are some on campus who jokingly exclaim that Marla has been at RCCC so long, that she helped 'pour the foundation' for the first building on campus. Marla has long served as Lillian's mentor; in fact, she is the mentor who encouraged Lillian to apply to RCCC. Because of her power and authority, she is incredibly influential. Marla literally knows every full-time faculty, staff, and administrator on campus, a fact she is quick to remind others of if they try to circumvent her authority. Marla is resistant to change, and thinks that Rock Creek is a great institution and a staple in the community. She isn't too fond of Red Valley University. Marla thinks faculty members there have become elitist and look down on RCCC students. She believes Red Valley's focus on research has caused the institution to forget its mission of serving the region. She believes Rock Creek students would be better served at other four year institutions that have a teaching focus. Marla and Lillian are both very committed to helping the students of Rock Creek achieve, but have varying opinions on how to accomplish that.

STATEMENT OF THE PROBLEM

As noted, Lillian is interested in positioning herself for the Vice President of Student Services position. Despite her prior success, a few members of the board of trustees have said that Lillian lacks the finesse for development, an emerging but crucial aspect of the role. If Lillian can orchestrate the team effort needed to accomplish the initiatives, she knows she will be a prime candidate for the position. Due to recent budget cuts, what could possibly be several million in endowed funds from Alexandra Nichols is vital to organization sustainability. More importantly, several RCCC board members have been critical of the institution's inability to establish a guaranteed transfer program. They are placing a lot of pressure on the President, who is placing a lot of pressure on Lillian and Chad. After seven years as a Dean, Lillian believes that she has earned the opportunity to compete for a Vice Presidency; she believes this is her chance.

Other than Chad, the rest of the committee is unaware of the potential monetary gift. The President of Rock Creek and the Board of Trustees have decided not to make public the potential gift. They are worried that if it is announced and not secured, it would be more detrimental than waiting for confirmation to announce. Preparing students to meet the criteria established by Red Valley is going to be challenging, at best. Currently, RCCC course reductions have lessened the likelihood that students can get all of their coursework completed within the identified timeframe, especially considering that most RCCC students are part-timers. Many RCCC faculty offer 'pet' courses which cover very interesting topics, but do not align with Red Valley's general education expectations (a likely rationale for the low course transfer rate). Finally, only a handful of RCCC faculty members are engaged in research. In fact, many work at RCCC because they prefer to teach instead of conducting research. Thus, providing students with exposure to research opportunities will also be challenging as it is antithetical to the organizational culture and mission. Moreover, professors taking time off for research could negatively impact class availability, prolonging the time it takes students to get necessary courses. In order to address these challenges, Lillian and Chad outline a plan. This plan does not apply to non-credit and certificate programs. Given that the plan is focused on curricular changes, this plan will then need to be shepherded through the faculty governance process by faculty leaders. Buy-in is key, as some faculty may want to protest any administrative 'tentacles in faculty affairs.' The following plan is devised:

- Eliminate the offering of *all* courses which do not transfer from all associate degree curricula.
- Increase all impacted course offerings (courses with high enrollment) equivalent to the space provided through the elimination of non-transfer courses.
- Require all general education courses to be offered in hybrid and online models (this will allow for larger course sections and free up faculty time).
- Require half of major-specific courses to be offered in hybrid format.
- Provide weekly technology training seminars for faculty; make attendance at two sessions per semester mandatory.
- Require each department to offer research opportunities for students in 10% of their courses.
- Beginning in two years, require faculty members to engage in research, with at least one conference presentation or publication annually.

HIGHLIGHTS OF FIRST COMMITTEE MEETING DISCUSSION

At the first committee meeting, Chad suggests that the institution move towards more hybrid (half online, half in-person) course offerings. Professors could serve more students by providing on- line course materials and interactions. This would allow for more course sections to be offered, reducing the negative effect of limited classroom space. Hybrid courses would save the institution money over time by decreasing per student expenditure costs and increasing revenue by raising enrollment opportunities. Chad recognizes that an enrollment increase could put a strain on the already small admission staff that Lillian is responsible for, but they both contend this is not a problem. Switching to an on-line model would require retrofitting to existing technology and would necessitate substantial teacher training. Further, shifting to this model could prove even more difficult for older faculty (50 years of age and older) who represent a large contingent of RCCCs faculty. If Chad can convince the faculty to get on board without forcing their hand, he will receive recognition from the President and Board for the cost savings. Chad has his sights set on a presidency and wants to enhance his professional credibility through this effort. Chad is very much against providing research opportunities so that students can get the necessary exposure. Research must be funded and faculty must have sufficient time to complete it. Research doesn't make sense to Chad given Rock Creek's current financial state. However, since he is part of the team proposing the plan, Chad is reluctantly on board with this item.

Diana isn't against the hybrid model, but she doesn't want to support the hybrid option since it was proposed by Chad. Because she is supportive of Lillian and her initiative, she won't fight Chad's proposal… *too* much. Diana's issue with hybrid model is that it will increase general education offerings, reducing the total 'pet' courses that many faculty currently offer. She's concerned about what that will do to the morale of the teachers. Diana is open to the research suggestion, believing that core faculty in each department should be left to determine how *research* will be implemented. She thinks that research opportunities may curb faculty member's angst about losing 'pet' classes, but she's not sure how to implement it. Diana is also concerned that more hybrid offerings design to increase course flow will inevitably result in a greater student enrollment. She believes that this will in fact reduce institutional quality. Further she thinks that teachers are too busy to handle more students. Overall, Diana likes the idea of institutional change, but is afraid too much change too quickly might stretch the teachers thin. She determines she can support Chad's proposal if Chad can agree to lower the pupil to professor ratio. Enrollment has made a steady climb recently and Diana believes that it is detrimental to faculty satisfaction. Lowering the ratio would give Diana a small win for the faculty, and may give her the support she needs to make a successful run at the Vice President of Academic Affairs position when Chad leaves.

Marla is not pleased with the proposal. Marla thinks change should be done incrementally over time, like a 'breeze' as opposed to the 'hurricane' that Chad and Lillian are suggesting. She is not interested in learning the technology associated with presenting hybrid classes. In fact, she detests hybrid courses, believing that face-to-face courses are the *only* way to go. Marla does not believe there is anything wrong with the way classes are being taught now. She is also very much against making the faculty give up their 'pet' classes. Pet classes hold high intrinsic value for the faculty. In fact, Marla is particularly proud of her own special courses. These courses allow professors to teach on topics they are passionate about. Marla isn't sure how much value 'research' will hold for students in the 'real-world.' She isn't a fan of Red Valley University imposing their research values on RCCC; values which she believes run contrary to the workforce development mission and very soul of the community college. What Marla is really concerned about is the percentage of adjunct faculty teaching at Rock Creek. There seems to be fewer and fewer full-time faculty, and when they retire, they are never replaced. Those she represents in the union are voicing concerns over the lack of full-time faculty. Marla is willing to help with the initiative if an agreement can be reached about increasing full-time, tenure track positions. Marla is willing to make concessions to accommodate the plan *if* full-time positions can be increased. Her fallback plan is to suggest that the plan is a collective bargaining issue and drastically halt further discussion. Reaching an agreement for full-time faculty would reify Marla's place as the most powerful faculty member on campus. Chad and Lillian are aware that they need Marla's help in getting buy-in from the faculty, and that the any proposed plan will fail without it.

Assume the role of Lillian. Your goal is to obtain the support to get the plan passed. Your next committee meeting is coming up in a week. What will you do?

Consider all of the power relationships in play, including your own when answering the following questions.

1.   What types of power are in play (legitimate, coercive, reward, expert, and referent)? How can you levy this power to achieve your goal?
2.   What should be your plan of attack to gain interest in pet classes, research, technological changes and the new class offering model?
3.   How can you use everyone's interest to your advantage? Consider the pros and cons of interests of your committee members.
4.   Come up with an all-encompassing proposal to be presented to the President and Board of Trustees with your recommendations on how to proceed.
5.   Create a brief presentation on how this experience has made you the ideal candidate for the Vice President of Student Services position.

CASE STUDY 10

INTERRUPTING EDUCATIONAL CAMPUS INEQUITIES

Lorri Johnson Santamaría

BACKGROUND

Pueblo Bonito College is a single campus public two-year community college. It is one of 108 colleges in the California Community Colleges system. It is one college in the largest community college district in the United States serving more than 250,000 students annually at nine colleges, spread throughout 36 cities in the greater Los Angeles area. The 200-acre main campus is nestled at the foot of the region's rolling inland hills and valleys in a lovely area approximately 30 miles east of the city of Los Angeles, and ten miles away from a major state supported public university. At Pueblo Bonito, students may choose from over 200 associate degree and certificate programs, complete the first two years of a bachelor's degree, or enjoy personal enrichment classes for lifelong learning.

Pueblo Bonito serves more than 30,000 full-time and part-time students each fall and spring semesters, while about 18,000 students attend during summer semester. Residents of California are charged an affordable $26 per unit. About 25 percent of the students are enrolled full-time, while about 60 percent are enrolled part-time in credit classes, and 15 percent are enrolled in non-credit classes.

Ethical Leadership and the Community College: Paradigms, Decision-Making, and Praxis,
pages 171–174.
Copyright © 2014 by Information Age Publishing

About half of the students are ages 18 through 24, while the other half are ages 24 through 60+. A majority of Pueblo Bonito students are employed. The student population is diverse in its ethnicity representative of the region, with over one-fourth Hispanic (28%), about six percent Asian, about four percent African American, and smaller populations of Filipino and Native American students. Another ten percent of enrolled students have not indicated their ethnicity, reflecting growing numbers of mixed race students. Pueblo Bonito typically serves approximately 300 international students from 49 different countries each semester. These students must achieve a minimum score of 470 on the Test of English as a Foreign Language and carry an F-1 student visa.

Academic achievement of students who are not White or Asian are consistent with national academic achievement gap trends nationwide. African American and Native American students are the most likely to drop out of the community college with the lowest grades. They are the lowest percentage of transfer rates to the University of California and California State University four-year state supported institutions. Hispanic students, mostly of Mexican descent, follow these same patterns of depressed academic achievement at Pueblo Bonito.

Although diversity and educational equity are core values reflected in the mission and vision of the college, the cultural and linguistic diversity of students is not reflected in the teaching faculty or administration at Pueblo. Nor are the students' multicultural multilingual identities acknowledged outside of the annual Unity in Diversity celebration hosted and organized by the EEO office. Predictably, over the past two academic years, there have been seven incidents described by campus police as hate-crimes involving race and gender, whereby students or faculty have been seriously threatened or hurt. Furthermore, the recent accreditation process revealed the need for the college to make immediate changes in hiring processes in order to diversify the faculty, staff, and administration at the college.

STATEMENT OF THE PROBLEM

In response to these developments, President Alicia Rodriguez initiated a nationwide search for a newly created position this spring. President Rodriguez has recently announced that you have been named associate vice president of diversity and educational equity and ombudsperson. You were chosen from a field of nearly 80 applicants, and were among the finalists who recently visited Pueblo Bonito for interviews and an open forum with members of the college community. Serving as the university's chief diversity officer, you will work with administration, faculty, staff and students to ensure that campus policies are inclusive and work towards stated commitments toward institutional diversity, social justice and equity. As ombudsperson, you will also serve as the designated impartial dispute resolution administrator, providing confidential and informal assistance to university constituents.

Your task is to address and interrupt educational inequities on your campus. In order to do this you must determine: (a) what kinds of resources will be allocated for this task; (b) your campus allies in this work; (c) what material disparities exist outside of the organization that impinge on the success of the college with regard to diversity initiatives; (d) a plan for dealing with the tension and challenge, requiring of moral courage and activism; and (e) a feasible measureable action plan.

The President suggests you meet with the office of advancement to develop a plan to 'raise friends' with a long-term goal to raise money to support diversity initiatives. You have a successful record with grant writing, however, and want to spend some time exploring grant and endowment opportunities as well. The President also suggests you identify a transition team to act as an advisory sounding board for a year. In reviewing the CVs and information on the transition team membership, you see that one of the individuals, the Dean of Sociology, has made significant contributions to diversity initiatives on campus, and who is strongly opposed to advancement of office goals. Other members of the team, including Chief of campus police, Deans of Education and Early Childhood Development, and the Native American Community Liaison, may not see eye to eye with regard to diversity on campus.

Patricia Daniels is the director of advancement. She feels that she knows how to convince individuals and families to support education, especially those of first generation students who are breaking cycles of poverty and are underrepresented. She is not sure how she feels regarding working directly on diversity initiatives. It doesn't feel right to her. She wants to be on the same page as the new hire yet, forcing square pegs into round holes has never been her area of expertise. She nervously prepares for her meeting with the new chief diversity officer, and hopes he does not invite her to sit on his transition team.

As the Education Dean, Charlie Harrison has a heart for diversity especially as it relates to addressing achievement gap issues. She is delighted she was invited to sit on the transition team, but wonders what kind of impact she will have in the diversity officer's thinking. He is likely to be focused on the big picture, where she knows the students by name wanting to become teachers some day to give back to the communities where they grew up. An active member of the Pauma band of Native Americans and a close friend of the Native American community liaison, Charlie is intent on making sure the new diversity officer is aware of the educational issues and challenges of all culturally and linguistically diverse students on campus. He also wants the diversity officer to be aware of the racial and ethnic diversity unique to students in 'Indian Country' and smaller populations on campus like African American students and mixed race students.

Narciso García is excited to have a chief officer of diversity and especially the ombudsperson role he is planning to take. As the campus police Chief, who also happens to be Puerto Rican, Narciso finds himself dragged into every other diversity-related dispute on campus, whether it be related to safety or crimes. Take last year; for example, when M.e.C.H.A was asked to move their Día de los

Muertos Celebration from the center of campus in front of the library to the fringe areas just outside of the main courtyard. Narciso was called to weigh in. The Dean of Associated Students was less concerned about safety and traffic than he was about having a cultural celebration front and center on campus outside of the Unity in Diversity spring event. Narciso showed up and let the ASI Dean know the celebration wasn't causing any safety issues, but from that day on Narciso has not been supported by the Dean. The campus police department has come under attack for not providing adequate police support for student events. Being able to talk this and similar situations over with an impartial party will be ideal. Narciso is happy to sit on the transition team, and hopefully gain an instant campus ally.

DISCUSSION QUESTIONS

1. What is the responsibility of the campus in providing a safe and supportive academic environment for student success?
2. What are the implications for the college and the surrounding region on student dropout?
3. In interrupting campus educational inequities, what resources are needed to facilitate improvements?
4. Is it reasonable to expect the diversity officer to comprehensively address campus inequities?

CASE STUDY 11

AM I REALLY GOING BACK TO SCHOOL?

JoLynn Langslet

BACKGROUND

Wood Valley Community College is a two-year college located in the Pacific Northwest. It is one of several community colleges located near a large metropolitan area with a population just under 600,000. Students who attend the college are drawn from both rural and metropolitan areas, and represent both traditional and non-traditional learners. The college mission is to serve the people of the college district with high quality education and opportunities that are accessible to all students, and adaptable to the changing needs of both the students and the community. In addition, the college has implemented a diversity action plan that seeks to maintain instructional and student support programs that recognize the diversity of its students and their unique needs. The diversity initiative was developed by the college administration due to student protest and unrest. Students' were upset about the lack of academic and social support afforded to students. They cite the dismal 18 percent graduation rate as benchmark for the institution not doing enough in facilitating academic success.

Ethical Leadership and the Community College: Paradigms, Decision-Making, and Praxis,
pages 175–177.
Copyright © 2014 by Information Age Publishing
All rights of reproduction in any form reserved.

Wood Valley offers a variety of transfer degrees, as well as more than 80 career and technical programs that range from short-term training to two-year associate degrees. Degree programs are offered on both traditional and non-traditional schedules and students can attend classes during the daytime, evenings, weekends, and over 5 week sessions.

Due to the recent changes in the economy and a demand for new jobs skills, Wood Valley, like many other community colleges, has seen a 27% increase in enrollment over the past year. In fact, the largest group represented in this increase is the non-traditional, or adult learner. Adult learners attending Wood Valley range from 25–55 years old. They are returning to school and seeking new skills for a variety of reasons including job competition, the need for higher wages, the desire for independence, and to start a new career. Most of these non-traditional students hold jobs in the workforce, and attend classes during evenings or weekends. In addition to working full-time, many of these students are parents and have numerous family responsibilities at home. There are a variety of needs unique to this specific group of students that can be challenging for the college and its support programs. For example, although the college offers a non-traditional class schedule, the operational hours for campus offices and support programs are during weekdays between 8:00am and 5:00pm. In addition, the majority of student clubs on campus are designed for and catered to the needs and lifestyles of the traditional student ages 18–24.

Due to recent budget constraints, there are little to no funds available for the operational expense of extending service hours or providing additional staff during evening or weekend hours. Furthermore, a recent survey conducted by the college administration on faculty and staff indicates strong resistance to offering student services beyond the traditional daytime hours, and very few faculty have indicated their willingness to teach during the hours that are required for a non-traditional program.

STATEMENT OF THE PROBLEM

You have recently been hired as the new Director for Student Services at Wood Valley Community College. You are responsible for overseeing all campus support programs for all student groups. Your first task, as directed from the office of the Vice President, is to evaluate the effectiveness and accessibility of campus resources and support programs for the growing number of non-traditional students. You are given one ten-week term to conduct and complete your evaluation. Consider the example below as you examine the information, identify problems, and consider various approaches that could resolve the issue(s).

Student Example:

Lucia Montoya is a 38-year old mother of two. She has been employed as a department store sales clerk for the past eight years, and is returning to school to learn new skills in order to change her career. Lucia is bilingual and desires to improve her spoken and written English skills in order to make her more competitive in the job market. During her first term at Wood Valley Community College, Lucia maintains her day job and commutes 40 minutes to attend evening classes twice a week. Although she would like to get involved with the campus bilingual club, the club meets only during weekday afternoons while Lucia is working. In addition, Lucia finds it difficult to access many of the campus support and service offices. She has been unable to resolve her financial aid matters since the financial aid office is only accessible during the day while she is working. She also wishes to utilize the career counseling office, but it is not available during the evening hours in which she is on campus to attend class. Lucia is frustrated and feels that her needs are not being met. She believes that the college has an obligation to address the needs of its non-traditional students, and not just the needs of the traditional, undergraduates. Lucia, along with many of her program peers who experienced the same frustrations, has voiced her concerns to the college administration and is seeking a timely resolution to these issues.

QUESTIONS TO CONSIDER

When considering the following questions, feel free to consider the challenges of adult learners at your own institution in providing context for similar issues at Wood Valley community college.

- What are the needs of the adult learners and what is the best way to assess those needs?
- What support programs and campus services are currently available to students and what is their accessibility?
- What are the responsibilities of the college in terms of providing support to adult learners, based on its mission statement and diversity action plan?
- What are the most time efficient and cost effective solutions to meet the unique needs of these students, while providing more resources as the program grows?

CASE STUDY 12

BONUS INCENTIVES FOR THE FORMER NBA STAR

Juanita Gamez Vargas

BACKGROUND

No-Name Community College (NNCC) is located in the western part of Oklahoma with a SMSA of 200,000. No-Name is the largest city within 100 miles of the nearest major city. NNCC is the only higher education institution in No-Name City. NNCC, established in 1972 by local community efforts, receives its funding through federal, state, and local taxes. NNCC enrolls an average of 6,000 full and part-time students and 10,000 continuing education students. The average student is 28 years old, married with 1.6 children, and reside in No-Name and the surrounding farming communities. Twenty-five percent of NNCC graduates transfer to Urban State College 100 miles away.

The state initially funded 75 percent of NNCC operating expenses, however, in the last 20 years, funding gradually declined to 35 percent. Today, state funding is at an all time low of 20 percent. The difference in funding comes from local county taxes and tuition increases. Committees formed in the last five years have assisted in identifying programs eliminated because of their lack of enrollment or replacement by newer technology. An early retirement incentives for faculty was

Ethical Leadership and the Community College: Paradigms, Decision-Making, and Praxis,
pages 179–181.
Copyright © 2014 by Information Age Publishing
179

initiated last year and vacancies are not filled when appropriate. For the last six years, employees have not received salary increases and merit raises were eliminated five years ago. Morale is low and faculty grumble about the lack of salary increases.

The NNCC Board is comprised of nine locally elected members, five women and four men. The Board president, Agnes Jolie, is the longest serving Board member. The other members represent small business owners and employees with the local oil and gas companies. Based on the recommendations by the faculty driven search committee, the NNCC board hired Dr. Amanda Chen eight months ago. Dr. Chen, formerly a chemistry instructor, had been VP for Instruction at an urban community college at a neighboring state. Dr. Chen's husband is Chief of Staff at No-Name Medical Center and their three children attend the local public schools. Dr. Chen's parents retired to No-Name to be close to the grandchildren. The Chens have enjoyed living in No-Name.

When Dr. Chen arrived at NNCC, several administrative changes had taken place. The VP for Instruction had left the state for a presidency and the VP for Student Services retired. Henry Hudson, VP for Business & Operating Services since 2007, remained and Dr. Chen found Henry informative and helpful during her transition. In the past eight months, Dr. Chen filled the VP for Instruction with Yvonna Fairbanks, a recent Ph. D. graduate from the Community College Leadership program in Kellogg, MI. Fairbanks had been Dean for Adult and Continuing Education at Kellogg (MI) Community College. Fairbanks' research interests were on budget and finance. She had written two successful multi-million dollar federal grants, and had served on several re-accreditation teams for the regional accreditation council. Her husband, Douglas Fairbanks, was the new president for First State Bank in No-Name.

Justin Longhair, a NNCC alumnus, was the new VP for Student Affairs. Justin and his wife, Emily, were originally from No-Name, but had been living in New York City (NYC) as Emily completed her studies at Columbia. Longhair had been director for international student services at a for-profit NYC college, a Fulbright scholar (China, 2008), and investment consultant for I. HaveMoney, Inc. Longhair's parents and siblings, all physicians, live in No-Name. Emily's parents also live in No-Name, and own a pharmaceutical company, Legit Drugs. Longhair's doctorate was on administrative corruption of student financial aid at community colleges. Longhair had published several articles based on his research while living in NYC. With their three children all in elementary school, the Longhair's decided it was time to leave the big city and be closer to family.

STATEMENT OF THE PROBLEM

One day as Dr. Chen is reviewing the budget with the business staff, she notices a check for $25,000 for the athletic director (AD), Kenny Star. When questioned, the payroll staff replies the check is an annual bonus "incentive" Star receives for not leaving the college. The president learns that Star, who oversees the men and women's basketball, baseball, and softball teams, was an NBA player in the late 1980s. Star, well liked in the community, owns several businesses and rental properties. Star started at NNCC in 1993 and for the first ten years drastically improved the basketball programs resulting in several state and national awards. Although the athletic programs have been increasing in operating expenses, winning has declined. As a result, attendance and sponsorships have declined as well. In fact, the administrative council had started discussing cutting the baseball and softball programs to curb expenses as recommended by Star. A sub-committee was formed to review such a proposal and compliance with Title IX.

Dr. Chen meets with VP Hudson and asks about the $25,000 annual bonus. Dr. Chen learns that the NNCC Foundation paid Star's bonus until 2001. Now the Student Services budget pays the bonus incentive because the Foundation is paying the mortgage for Star's lake house. These financial arrangements are a "gentleman's agreement" among the former community college president, foundation director, and Star. Hudson's predecessor developed a process for paying Star the incentive without drawing attention to a paper trail.

After thoughtful consideration of issues presented, reflect on how you could move forward and address these annual bonuses paid to Star. Consider the following:

- What strategies would you undertake to determine whether the bonus incentive was appropriate and/or within standard operating procedures and whether Star merited continuation of the bonus incentive?
- What about the Foundation's contributions to Star's lake house? How much is Star receiving from NNCC to remain at the institution?
- What information should you gather to determine whether these contributions are within the legal purview of the college's foundation?
- Who from your executive council would you include in your investigation and why? Who else should you enlist to assist you in this investigation and why?
- Even if the two financial incentives are legally appropriate, should you re-consider the "gentleman's agreement" given the financial constraints NNCC is experiencing.
- When should you discuss this issue with your Board? What factors would help you determine your recommendation?

REFERENCES

Abrahamson, K. (2006). The ethic of rationing education in the California community colleges. *eJournal of Education Policy*. Retrieved February 4, 2013, from: https://www4nau.edu/cee/jep/journal2006/paper7.htm.

American Association of Community Colleges (AACC, 2008). *About community colleges*. Retrieved from http://www.aacc.nche.edu/AboutCC/Pages/default.aspx.

Alemán Jr., E. (2007). Situating Texas school finance policy in a CRT framework: How "substantially equal" yields racial inequity. *Educational Administration Quarterly, 43*, 525–558.

Arthur, J. (1998). Communitarianism: What are the implications for education? *Educational Studies, 24*, 353–368.

Associated Press. (2006, October 2). Four going to jail for fraud at community college. Retrieved July 18, 2010, from: http://sports.espn.go.com/ncaa/news/story?id=2611020.

Astin, A. W. (1977). *Four critical years*. San Francisco: Jossey-Bass.

Astin, A. W. (1993). *What matters in college? Four critical years revisited*. San Francisco: Jossey-Bass.

Baker, G. A., III, Dudziak, J., & Tyler, P. (Eds.). (1994). *A handbook on the community college in America: Its history, mission, and management*. Westport, CT: Greenwood.

Baldwin, D. A. (2002). Power and international relations. In W. Carlsnaes, T. Risse, and B. A. Simmons (Eds)., *Handbook of international relations* (pp. 177–191). Sage Publications.

Barr, M. J., Desler, M. K. & Associates (Eds.), 2000. *The handbook of student affairs administration*. San Francisco, CA: Jossey-Bass.

Ethical Leadership and the Community College: Paradigms, Decision-Making, and Praxis, pages 183–190.

Beckner, W. (2004). *Ethics for educational leaders.* Boston, MA: Pearson.

Begley, P. T., & Stefkovich, J. (2007). Integrating values and ethics into postsecondary teaching for leadership development: Principles, concepts, and strategies. *Journal of Educational Administration, 45*(4), 398–412.

Bell, D. (2010). Communitarianism. In. E. N. Zalta (Ed.), *The Stanford encyclopedia of philosophy.* Retrieved from: http://plato.stanford.edu/archives/fall2010/entries/communitarianism/.

Bentham, J. (1789). *Introduction to principles of morals and legislation.* Oxford, UK: Clarendon.

Beyerle, D. (2009, December 14). Two-year college scandal nearing end. *Tuscaloosa News.* Retrieved July 18, 2010, from: http://www.tidesports.com/article/20091214/NEWS/912139939?p=5&tc=pg.

Blanchard, K. H., & Peale, N. V. (1988). *The power of ethical management.* New York, NY: W. Morrow.

Blum, L. A. (1988). Gilligan and Kohlberg: Implications for moral theory. *Ethics, 98*(3), 472–491.

Bogue, J. P. (1950). *The community college.* New York, NY: McGraw-Hill.

Bohman, J. (2005). *Critical Theory.* In E. N. Zalta (Ed.), *The Stanford encyclopedia of philosophy.* Stanford, CA: Center for the Study of Language and Information, Stanford University. Retrievable from: http://plato.stanford.edu/archives/spr2013/entries/critical-theory/.

Bourdieu, P. (1988). *Homo academicus.* Oxford: Polity Press.

Bourdieu, P. (1990). *In other words: Essays towards a reflexive sociology.* Cambridge: Polity Press.

Bourdieu, P. (1997). Selections from the logic of practice. In A. D. Schrift (Ed.), *The logic of the gift* (pp. 190–230). New York: Routledge.

Bourdieu, P. (2001). The forms of capital. In J. Richardson (Ed.), *Handbook of theory and research for the sociology of education.* Westport, CT: Greenwood Press.

Bourdieu, P. (2003). *The social structures of the economy.* Cambridge: Polity Press.

Bourdieu, P., & Passeron, J. C. (1990). *Reproduction in education, society and culture.* Thousand Oaks: Sage Publications.

Bourdieu, P. (2005 [2000]). *The social structures of the economy* (Chris Turner, Trans.). Cambridge: Polity Press.

Bourdieu, P. & Wacquant, L. J. D. (1992). *An invitation to reflexive sociology.* Chicago: The University of Chicago Press.

Bowen, S. A. (2005). A practical model of ethical decision making in issues management and public relations. *Journal of Public Relations Research, 17*(3), 191–216.

Caldwell, C., Shapiro, J. P., & Gross, S. J. (2007). Ethical leadership in higher education admission: Equality vs. equity. *Journal of College Admission,* 14–19.

Calhoun, C, J., Gerteis, J., Moody, J., Pfaff, S., & Virk, I. (2002). *Contemporary sociological theory.* Boston, MA: Blackwell Publishing.

Carr, A. (2000). Critical theory and the management of change in organizations. *Journal of Organizational Change Management, 13*(3), 208–220.

Cicero (1913), De Officiis (W. Miller, Trans.). Cambridge, MA: Harvard.

Chryssides, G., & Kaler, J. (1996). *Essentials of business ethics.* London: McGraw-Hill.

Ciulla, J. B. (2003). *The ethics of leadership.* Stamford, CT: Cengage Learning.

Cohen, A. M. (2001). Governmental policies affecting community colleges: A historical perspective. In B. K. Townsend & S. B. Twombly (Eds.), *Community colleges: Policy in the future context* (pp. 3–22). Westport, CT: Ablex.

Cohen, A. M., & Brawer, F. B. (2003). *The American community college,* (4th Ed.). San Francisco, CA: Jossey-Bass.

Collins, J. (1993). Determination and Contradiction: An appreciation and critique of the work of Pierre Bourdieu on Language and Education. In P. Bourdieu, C. J. Calhoun, E. Lipuma, & M. Postone (Eds.), *Bourdieu: Critical perspectives* (pp. 116–138). Chicago: University of Chicago Press.

Dalton, J. C., Crosby, P. C., Valente, A., & Eberhardt, D. (2009). Maintaining and modeling everyday ethics in student affairs. In G. S. McClellan & J. String (Eds.), *The handbook of student affairs administration* (pp. 166–186). San Francisco, CA: Jossey-Bass.

Delgado, R. (1995). *Critical race theory: The cutting edge.* Philadelphia: Temple University.

Dewey, R. E., Gramlich, F. W., & Loftsgordon, D. (1961). *Problems of ethics.* New York, NY: Macmillan.

Doscher, S. P., & Normore, A. H. (2005). Feminine concepts of leadership and power: A new framework for development ethics and education development. *Proceedings of the Florida International University College of Education Research Conference, 9–14.* Retrieved from: http://education.fiu.edu/research_conference/docs/proceedings/2005_COERC_Proceedings.pdf#page=23.

Driver, J. (2009). The history of Utilitarianism. In E. N. Zalta (Ed.), *The Stanford encyclopedia of philosophy.* Retrieved from: http://plato.stanford.edu/entries/utilitarianism-history/.

Dupré, B. (2007). *Fifty philosophy ideas you really need to know.* Teaticket, MA: Quercus.

Eells, W. C. (1931). *The junior college.* Boston, MA: Houghton Mifflin.

Eells, W. C. (1941). *Present status of the junior college terminal education.* Washington, DC: American Association of Junior Colleges.

Enomoto, E. K. (1997). Negotiating the ethics of care and justice. *Educational Administration Quarterly, 33*(3), 351–370.

Etzioni, A. (2003). Communitarianism. In K. Christensen & D. Levinson (Eds.), *Encyclopedia of community: From the village to the virtual world* (pp. 224–228). Thousand Oaks, CA: SAGE.

Fletcher, J. (1966). *Situation ethics: The new morality.* Philadelphia, PA: Westminster.

Fujimoto, E. O. (2012). Hiring diverse faculty members in community colleges: A case study in ethical decision making. *Community College Review, 40*(3), 255–274.

French, J., & Raven, B. (1959). The bases of social power. In D. Cartwright (Ed.), *Studies in social power* (pp. 150–167). Ann Arbor, MI: University of Michigan.

Furman, G. C. (2003). Moral leadership and the ethic of community. *Values and ethics in educational administration, 2*(1), 1–8.

Furman, G. C. (2004). The ethic of community. *Journal of Educational Administration, 42*(2), 215–235.

Futrell, M. (1999). The challenge of the 21st century: Developing a highly qualified cadre of teachers to teach our nation's diverse student population. *Journal of Negro Education, 68*(3), 318–334.

George, M. (2010). Ethics and motivation in remedial mathematics education. *Community College Review, 38*(1), 82–92.

Gilligan, C. (1977). In a different voice: Women's conceptions of self and of morality. *Harvard Educational Review, 47*(4), 481–517.

Gilligan, C. (1982). *In a different voice: Psychological theory and women's development.* Cambridge, MA: Harvard University.

Gilligan, C. (1995). Hearing the difference: Theorizing connection. *Hypatia, 10*(2), 120–127.

Giroux, H. A. (1988). *Teachers as intellectuals: Towards a critical pedagogy of learning.* Westport, CT: Greenwood.

Gleazer, E. J. (1994). Evolution of junior colleges into community colleges. In G. A. Baker III, J. Dudziak & P. Tyler (Eds.), *A handbook on the community college in America: Its history, mission, and management* (pp. 17–27). Westport, CT: Greenwood.

Goldberg, M. E. (2000, May). An interview with Carol Gilligan: Restoring lost voices. *Phi Delta Kappan,* 701–704.

Grenfell, M., James, D., Hodkinson, P., Reay, D., & Robbins, D. (1998). *Acts of practical theory: Bourdieu and education.* Milton Park: Falmer Press.

Harris, B. W. (2013). Staying focused on the agenda: The greatest challenge in a complex environment. *Journal of Transformative Leadership and Policy Studies, 3*(1), 57–59.

Helkama, K. (2004) Values, role-taking and empathy in moral development, *New Review of Social Psychology,* 3(1–2), 103–111.

Horkheimer, M. (1982). *Critical theory.* New York, NY: Seabury.

Horkheimer, M. (1993). *Between philosophy and social science.* Cambridge, MA: MIT press.

Jay, M. (1973). *The dialectical imagination: A history of the Frankfurt school and the institute of social research.* Boston, MA: Little, Brown, and Company.

Jos, P. H., & Hines, S. M. (1993). Care, justice, and public administration. *Administration and Society, 25*(3), 373–392.

Juujärvi, S. (2006) The ethic of care development: a longitudinal study of moral reasoning among practical-nursing, social-work and law-enforcement students, *Scandinavian Journal of Psychology, 47*(3), 193–202.

Kant, I. (1996). *Critique of pure reason.* Indianapolis, IN: Hackett.

Kellner, D. (2003). Toward a critical theory of education. *Democracy & Nature, 9*(1), 51–64.

Kincheloe, J. L., & McLaren, P. (2002). Rethinking critical theory and qualitative research. In Y. Zou & E. T. Trueba (Eds.), *Ethnography and schools: Qualitative approaches to the study of education* (pp. 87–138). Oxford, UK: Rowman and Littlefield.

Kohlberg, L. (1973). The claim of moral adequacy of a highest stage of moral judgment. *The Journal of Philosophy, 70*(18), 630–646.

Kohlberg, L. (1980). Educating for a just society. In B. Munsey, B. (Ed.), *Moral development, moral education, and Kohlberg* (pp. 455–471). Birmingham, AL: Religious Education Press.

Kohlberg, L. (1981). *Essays on moral development* (Vol. 1). New York, NY: Harper & Row.

Kohlberg, L. (2008). The development of children's orientations toward a moral order: Sequence in the development of moral thought. *Human Development, 51,* 9–20.

Krupnick, M. (2007, June 15). Grades scandal hits other campus: Administrators admit that scheme to change marks for money affected Los Medanos College as well as Diablo Valley. *Contra Costa Times.* Retrieved July 18, 2010, from: http://www.contracostatimes.com/ci_6073213?source=pkg&nclick_check=1.

Krupnick, M. (2008, March 5). Assembly responds to DVC scandal: Bill promoting security of college grades advances. *State Digest.* Retrieved July 18, 2010, from: http://democrats.assembly.ca.gov/members/a18/News_Room/News/20080305AD18AR01.aspx.

Lamont, J., & Favor, C. (2013). Distributive justice. In. E. N. Zalta (Ed.), *The Stanford encyclopedia of philosophy.* Retrieved from: http://plato.stanford.edu/entries/justice-distributive/.

Langlois, L., & Begley, P. (2005). *Mapping out literature and research on ethics and valuation.* University Park, PA: Willower Center for the Study of Leadership and Ethics, Pennsylvania State University.

Lee, H. K. (2007, August, 16). New Diablo Valley College leader stresses integrity after scandal. *San Francisco Chronicle.* Retrieved July 18, 2010, from: http://www.cal-state.edu/pa/clips2007/august/16aug/diablo.shtml.

Levanthal, G. S. (1980). What should be done with equity theory? *Social Exchange, 27*–55.

Levinson, M. (2007). *The civic achievement gap: Circle working paper 51.* College Park, MD: The Center for Information and Research on Civic Learning and Engagement.

Marx, K. (1978). *The poverty of philosophy.* Moscow: Progress.

Marx, K., & Engels, F. (1848/1999). *The Communist manifesto.* New York, NY: St. Martin's.

Maxcy, S. J. (2002). *Ethical school leadership.* Lanham, MD: Rowan and Littlefield.

McClenney, K. M. (2007). Research update: The community college survey of student engagement. *Community College Review, 35*(2), 137–146.

McFarlane, B. (2001). Justice and lectures professionalism. *Teaching in Higher Education, 6*(2), 141–152.

McLaren, P. (1995). *Critical pedagogy and predatory culture: Oppositional politics in a postmodern era.* New York, NY: Routledge.

McLaren, P. 2003. Critical pedagogy: A look at the major concepts. In A. Darder, M. Baltodano, & R. D. Torres (Eds.), *The critical pedagogy reader* (pp. 69–96).New York: RoutledgeFalmer.

Medsker, L. L. (1960). *The junior college: Progress and prospect.* New York, NY: McGraw-Hill.

Messina, K. (2006). The ethical dilemma of increasing the part time faculty load to 80% at California community colleges. *eJournal of Education Policy.* Retrieved January 11, 2013 from: https://www4.nau.edu/cee/jep/journal2006/paper6.htm

Mill, J. S. (1863/2003). What utilitarianism is. In J. B. Ciulla (Ed.), *The ethics of leadership* (pp. 143–151). Belmont, CA: Wadsworth Cengage.

Mills, K. (2003, Winter). Community college baccalaureates: Some critics decry the trend as "mission creep." *National CrossTalk.* Retrieved from http://www.highereducation.org/crosstalk/ct0103/news0103-community.shtml.

Monroe, C. R. (1977). *Profile of the community college.* San Francisco, CA: Jossey-Bass.

Murray, S. J. (2009). Aporia: towards an ethic of critique. *Aporia, 1*(1), 8–14.

Mytelka, A. (2007, September, 26). Guilty plea in grade-changing scandal at 2-year college in California. *The Chronicle of Higher Education.* Retrieved July 18, 2010, from: http://chronicle.com/article/Guilty-Plea-in-Grade-Changing/39641/

Nagel, T. (1973). Rawls on justice. *Philosophical Review, 82*, 228–234.

Nevarez, C., & Wood, J. L. (2010). *Community college leadership and administration: Theory, practice, and change.* New York, NY: Peter Lang.

Nevarez, C., & Wood, J. L. (2012). A case study framework for community college leaders. *Community College Journal of Research and Practice, 36,* 310–316.

Nevarez, C., Wood, J. L., & Penrose, R. (2013). *Leadership theory and the community college: Applying theory to practice.* Sterling, VA: Stylus.

Noddings, N. (2003). *Caring: A feminine approach to ethics and moral education* (2nd ed.). Berkeley, CA: University of California.

Noddings, N. (2008). Care and moral education. In H S. Shapiro & D. E. Purpel (Eds.), *Critical social issues in American education: Democracy and meaning in a globalizing world* (pp. 291–302). Mahwah, NJ: Lawrence Erlbaum.

Northouse, P. G. (2007). *Leadership theory and practice.* London, UK: Sage.

Oliver, D. E., & Hioco, B. (2012). An ethical decision-making framework for community college administrators. *Community College Review, 40*(3), 240–254.

Olsen, J. (1997). Theories of justice and their implications for priority setting in health care. *Journal of Health Economy, 17,* 625–640.

Patton, J. (1998). The disproportionate representation of African Americans in special education: Looking behind the curtain for understanding and solutions. *The Journal of Special Education, 32*(1), 25–31.

Pratt, M. W., Skoe, E. E. A., & Arnold, M. L. (2004). Care reasoning development and family socialisation patterns in later adolescence: A longitudinal analysis. *International Journal of Behavioral Development, 28*(2), 139–147. doi: 10.1080/01650250344000343

Ramose, M. B. (1999). *African philosophy through Ubuntu.* Harare, ZI: Mond Books.

Rand, A. (1961). *The virtue of selfishness.* New York, NY; Penguin.

Rand, A. (1959). *Atlas shrugged.* New York, NY: Random House.

Ratcliff, J. L. (1994). Seven streams in the historical development of the modern American community college. In G. A. Baker III, J. Dudziak, & P. Tyler (Eds.), *A handbook on the community college in America: Its history, mission, and management* (pp. 3–16). Westport, CT: Greenwood Press.

Raven, B. &, French, J. R.P. (1959). *Bases of social power.* Cartwright. University of Michigan, Ann Arbor.

Rawls, J. (2003). Distributive justice. In J. B. Ciulla (Eds.), *The ethics of leadership* (pp. 154–161). Belmont, CA: Wadsworth. [Reprinted from Rawls, J. (1967). Distributive justice. In P. Laslett. & W. G. Runciman (Eds.), *Philosophy, politics, and society* (pp. 58–82). New York, NY: Harper and Row].

Richardson R. C. Jr. (1987). The presence of access and the pursuit of achievement. In J. S. Eaton (Ed.)., *Colleges of choice: The enabling impact of the community college* (pp. 25–46). New York: Macmillan.

Robbins, S., & Trabichet, L. (2009). Ethical decision-making by educational leaders: Its foundations, culture and more recent perspectives. *Management in Education, 23*(2), 51–56.

Roubanis, J. L., Garner, S. F., & Purcell, R. S. (2008). Professionalism: Ethical decision making as a foundation for professional practice. *Journal of Family Consumer Sciences Education, 26*(2), 44–59.

Sabbagh, C. (2001). A taxonomy of normative and empirically oriented theories of distributive justice. *Social Justice Research, 14*(3), 237–263.

Shapiro, J. P. (2006). Ethical decision making in turbulent times: Bridging theory with practice to prepare authentic educational leaders. *Values and ethics in educational administration, 4*(2), 1–8.

Shapiro, J. P., & Gross, S. J. (2008). Ethical educational leadership in turbulent times: (Re) solving moral dilemmas. New York, NY: Lawrence Erlbaum Associates.

Shapiro, J. P., & Hassinger, R. E. (2007). Using case studies on ethical dilemmas for the development of moral literacy: Towards educating for social justice. *Journal of Educational Administration, 45*(4), 451–470.

Shapiro, H. S., & Purpel, D. E. (Eds) (2004). *Critical social issues in American education: Democracy and meaning in a globalized world* (3rd ed). Mahwah, NJ: Lawrence Erlbaum.

Shapiro, J. P., & Stefkovich, J. A. (2005). *Ethical leadership and decision making in education: Applying theoretical perspectives to complex dilemmas* (2nd ed). Mahwah, NJ: Lawrence Erlbaum.

Simola, S. (2003). Ethics of justice and care in corporate crisis management. *Journal of Business Ethics, 46*(4), 351–361.

Skoe, E. E. A. (1998) The ethic of care: issues in moral development, in: E. E. Aspaas Skoe & A. L. von der Lippe (Eds.), *Personality development in adolescence: A cross national and life span perspective* (pp. 143–171). London: Routledge.

Skoe, E. E. A. (2010). The relationship between empathy-related constructs and care-based moral development in young adulthood. *The Journal of Moral Development, 39*(2), 191–211. doi: 10.1080/03057241003754930

Skoe, E. E. A., Cumberland, A., Eisenberg, N., Hansen, K., & Perry, J. (2002). The influences of sex and gender-role identity on moral cognition and prosocial personality traits. *Sex Roles, 46*(9–10), 295–309.

Skoe, E. E., & Marcia, J. E. (1991). A care-based measure of morality and its relation to ego identity. *Merrill-Palmer Quarterly, 37*, 289–304.

Skoe, E. E. A., & von der Lippe, A. L. (2002). Ego development and the ethics of care and justice: The relations among them revisited. *Journal of Personality, 70*(4), 485–508.

Sleeter, C. (1996). Multicultural education as a social movement. *Theory into Practice 35*,(4), 239–247.

Starrat, R. J. (1991). Building an ethical school: A theory for practice in educational leadership. *Educational Administration Quarterly, 27*(2), 185–202.

Starratt, R. J. (2004). *Ethical leadership.* San Francisco, CA: Jossey-Bass.

St. John, E. (2009). *College organization and professional development: Integrating moral reasoning in reflective practice.* New York, NY: Routledge.

Strike, K. A. (2007). *Ethical leadership in schools: Creating community in an environment of accountability.* Thousand Oaks, CA: Corwin.

Strike, K. A., Haller, E. J., & Soltis, J. F. (2005). *The ethics of school administration* (3rd ed.). New York: Teachers College Press

Sucher, S. J. (2008). *The moral leader: Challenges, tools, and insights.* New York, NY: Routledge.

Taylor, S. (2010, January 26). Two arrested in college scandal. *Tuscaloosa News.* Retrieved July 18, 2010, from: http://www.tidesports.com/article/20091214/NEWS/912139939?p=5&tc=pg.

Thernbon, G. (1996). Dialectics of modernity: On critical theory and the legacy of twentieth century Marxism. *New Left Review, 215*(1), 59–81.

Tillery, D., & Deegan, W. L. (1985). *Renewing the American community college.* San Francisco, CA: Jossey-Bass.

Tinto, V. (1987). *Leaving college: Rethinking the causes and cures of student attrition* (1st ed.). Chicago: University of Chicago Press.

Van Staveren, I. (2007). Beyond utilitarianism and deontology: Ethics in economics. *Review of Political Economy, 19*(1), 21–35.

Vaughan, G. B. (1983). Introduction: Community colleges in perspective. In G. B. Vaughan (Ed.), *Issues for community college leaders in a new era* (pp. 1–20). San Francisco, CA: Jossey-Bass.

Vaughan, G. B. (1992). *Dilemmas of leadership: Decision making and ethics in the community college.* San Francisco, CA: Jossey-Bass.

Vaughan, G. B. (2006). *The community college story* (3rd ed.). Washington, DC: Community College Press.

Velasquez, M., Moberg, D., Meyer, M. J., Shanks, T., McLean, M. R., Decosse, D., André, C., & Hanson, K. O. (2009). *A framework for thinking ethically.* Santa Clara, CA: Markkula Center for Applied Ethics, Santa Clara University.

Vernez, G., & Mizell, L. (2001). *GOAL: To double the rate of Hispanics earning a bachelor's degree.* Santa Monica, CA: RAND.

Vogel, L. R. (2012). Leading with hearts and minds: Ethical orientations of educational leadership doctoral students. *Values and ethics in educational administration, 10*(1), 1–12.

West, H. R. (2004). An introduction to Mill's Utilitarian ethics. Cambridge, UK: Cambridge University.

Wilson, F. (2007). John Stuart Mill. In. E. N. Zalta (Ed.), *The Stanford encyclopedia of philosophy*. Retrieved from: http://www.science.uva.nl/~seop/entries/mill/.

Woolfolk, A. (2008). *Educational psychology: Active learning edition* (10th ed.). San Francisco, CA: Pearson.

Yukl, G. (1994). *Leadership in organizations* (3rd ed.). Englewood Cliffs, NJ; Prentice Hall.

Wood, J. L., & Harris III, F. (2013). The Community College Survey of Men: An initial validation of the instrument's non-cognitive outcomes construct. *Community College Journal of Research and Practice, 37*, 333–338.

Wood, J. L. & Hilton, A. A. (2012). Five ethical paradigms for community college leaders: Toward constructing and considering alternative courses of action in ethical decision making. *Community College Review, 40*(3), 196–214.

AUTHOR BIOGRAPHIES

J. Luke Wood is Assistant Professor of Administration, Rehabilitation, and Post-secondary Education and the Director of the Doctoral Program Concentration in Community College Leadership at San Diego State University (SDSU). Dr. Wood is also Co-Director of the Minority Male Community College Collaborative (M2C3), Chair of the Multicultural & Multiethnic Education (MME) special interest group of the American Educational Research Association (AERA), and Chair-Elect for the Council on Ethnic Participation (CEP) for the Association for the Study of Higher Education (ASHE).

Carlos Nevarez is the Director and a Full Professor for the Doctorate in Educational Leadership Program at California State University, Sacramento. Dr. Nevarez is also the Co-Founder and Executive Editor of the Journal of Transformative Leadership & Policy Studies. A nationally recognized leader, Dr. Nevarez has published numerous books and scholastic articles. He has been invited to speak as an expert on Leadership in Education, at summits and conferences throughout the United States.

Ethical Leadership and the Community College: Paradigms, Decision-Making, and Praxis,
pages 191.
Copyright © 2014 by Information Age Publishing

CPSIA information can be obtained at www.ICGtesting.com
Printed in the USA
LVOW04s1524140515

438487LV00001B/8/P